Decent and Indecent

Benjamin Spock, M.D.

Decent and Indecent

Our Personal and Political Behavior

The McCall Publishing Company • New York

To the young people, black and white,
who are being clubbed, jailed, and even killed
for showing us the way to justice.

Library of Congress Catalog Card Number: 75–97785

SBN 8415–0001–0

Printed in the United States of America

Contents

III. Aggression and Hostility

IV. The Psychology of Political Attitudes

Contents vii

V. Education for What?

Gratitude

After I finished the first draft of this manuscript three years ago I needed to find out what it meant to others. I feared that young people, whom I particularly wanted to reach, might find some of its philosophy too outdated to take seriously, so I sent fourteen copies to medical students and undergraduates at Western Reserve University. All of them weren't sure what the manuscript meant, and they disagreed with various parts, but none thought it foolish. I felt grateful for this amount of backing. They were Albert Alter, Juanita Bracale, Sally Bronson, Michael Decker, Michael Goldfein, Howard Kleckner, Carole Lauric, James McMillan, David Satcher, Lawrence Schonberger, Joyce Weinberger, Debbie Weisberger, Stephanie Wohl, Rhoda Yaner.

Next I got valuable comments from my favorite experts in psychiatry, sociology, and politics: Mary Bergen, Douglas Bond, Douglas Lenkoski, Leo Despres, Heather Booth, Paul Booth, and I. F. Stone.

I rewrote for two more years, in the hours I could find on planes, in airports, in hotels, on my sailboat as well as at home. Toward the end I received valuable editorial help from Robert Lescher, Robert Stein, and Byron Dobell. Norma Nero has typed the manuscript what must have seemed like dozens of times and has encouraged me often with her enthusiasm. Jane Spock deserves the most credit for being gracious about the hundreds of evenings when we gave up seeing friends, movies, and ballet while I wrote.

Preview

This book is about certain problems of modern Western man as I see them. They are:

A loss of a sense of direction or ideals that has had a demoralizing effect on various pursuits.

Increasing rivalry between the sexes, which is making both men and women dissatisfied with their roles.

An oversimplified concept of sexuality that impairs its dignity and its pleasures.

An ingenuous readiness to blame all our own aggressiveness and hatred on other people who don't belong to our particular group or nation, an attitude that, in a nuclear age, is pushing us inexorably to self-destruction.

The failure to find a political form that will enable the cooperative side of our natures to maintain the upper hand over our greed and power craving.

The difficulty, in an ever more technological age, of keeping education geared to our emotional, social, and spiritual needs.

These topics may sound so disparate as to hardly belong under one title. But from my viewpoint there is a common theme that is all-important: These particular difficulties are caused primarily by a lack of understanding of our deeper human motivations—conscious and unconscious. We mislead ourselves by assuming that the judgments and courses of action we come to are based on reasoning whereas they are often quite irrational and even self-defeating. Nevertheless, these deeper drives do follow patterns that have been analyzed and explained, first by Freud. So we could anticipate and control our inappropriate reactions if we would be willing to look at them more honestly and critically, which is what this book is about.

To put it more personally and more sharply, I've spent my life studying and advising how to bring up children to be well adjusted and happy. Now I see the futility of such efforts if these children are then to be incinerated in an imbecilic war, or if, when grown, they find life disillusioning because the society they inherit is confused about sex and gender and brutality, is perverted in its internal and external aims by power-obsessed leaders, and seems oblivious of the loving and creative potentialities of our species.

A worry I have had in writing this book is that my own particular ideals and standards might seem so old-fashioned and strict to some readers—especially young ones—that they would not bother to judge the general psychological concepts behind the specifics but might reject them out of hand. Young people today, because of the pervasive hypocrisies of our society, reject as arbitrary and unproven all sorts of doctrines of restraint with much greater vehemence than any previous generation did. This fear of mine applies particularly to my ideas about the harm from uncontrolled obscenity, about the likelihood of feelings of sexual inhibition in young people raised with strict standards, and about the temperamental differences between the sexes.

My aim is not to recommend my own particular morals or solutions but to point out psychological truths, though it is difficult for anyone to be sure he has succeeded in keeping such distinctions.

To make my potential biases clear I'll explain that I was brought up in a family with stern morals even by New England standards and acquired an oppressive conscience. I tried to free myself from these throughout adolescence and young adulthood, believing then that a knowledge of biology, psychology, and sociology should offer sufficient guides for a modern man. But I found that it is impossible to shuck one's character. Recently I've come to realize that the worst problems of America—illegal war, racial injustice, unnecessary poverty, for example—are caused not by lack of knowledge or means but by moral blindness or confusion. So I have come full circle, in the end, to a feeling that it is crucial, in all issues, to consider the moral dimension.

I

Where Does Idealism Come From?

This part is about man's idealism and spirituality and creativity—which were often called his soul in former times. Increasingly, over the past hundred years, man has acted as if he had lost his belief in these values and in his own worth and dignity. Is there any reality in the concepts of idealism and spirituality? What is their origin, psychologically speaking?

Disillusionment

Most Americans who consider themselves thinking people are disillusioned, I believe, but are not conscious of this feeling. They are not disenchanted with the physical aspects of civilization. They are proud of space ships and artificial heart valves. What they have lost is a belief in the dignity of man.

The trend probably started earlier, but it became obvious in the disillusionment of writers, artists, and other intellectuals which followed World War I. In the 1920s there came an insistent "debunking" of history: biographers emphasized the stupid, ridiculous, or immoral aspects of our heroes. Novels and plays became increasingly cynical. In recent years they have gone on to emphasize the crude, animal aspects of men and women, as if to say, "This is what people are really like. The rest is sham." A highly admired recent play consisted largely of a husband's and wife's contemptuous revelations of each other's repulsive characteristics.

Paintings used to show people who were pleasing to look at. Now if human beings are painted at all they are ugly and distorted. Modern dance uses gestures that in the past would have been called angry or awkward. Serious music has shifted from consonant to dissonant, as if only the harsher sounds are meaningful. I'm not trying to judge the excellence or permanence of today's arts or

3

saying that what preceded them was better. Arts must develop or peter out. I'm only pointing to the common denominator of our disbelief in what was previously considered admirable in human nature.

A person expresses his regard for those he associates with—and also for himself—by his clothes and grooming. Since the turn of the century there has been a progressive retreat from formality. By the late 1950s there appeared a deliberate slovenliness that expressed, I think, a scorn for self as well as for others. I saw medical students come to clinics to meet their patients in rumpled, soiled, old clothes that would be more appropriate for cleaning the cellar. (The anticonventional and impoverished hippie look represents, in addition, a rejection of society's materialism.)

There has been a trend in social gatherings to substitute loud joshing and playful insults for conversation and to use crude expressions in place of traditional ones. Husbands and wives often pretend, in company, to have less respect for each other than they actually feel—the opposite of the manners of the past. I'm not against good parties or even wild parties. I'm only asking why people are trying to impress each other with how coarse they can be.

Greeting cards formerly carried kindly sentiments. Now they hoot at the invalid or birthday celebrator, who is pictured as obese, hairy, and warty.

You can see in some of these examples that along with man's self-depreciation there is a considerable release of hostility and an impulse to knock standards down. Frank expression of this has occurred in staged "happenings," such as the one in which the performers smashed a piano to kindling with axes and plastered a naked girl with spaghetti, which she then hurled at the audience, while six radios tuned to different stations played at top volume. This represents emotional regression all the way back to the one-to-two-year-old level, when the child in a spell of anger wants to antagonize and mess and destroy on a titanic scale. It also indicates deep uncertainty regarding human destiny, to put it mildly.

In earlier centuries man considered himself a unique being whom God had created in His image. Part of the respect he had for God he also felt for himself as God's special creation. The discovery of evolution persuaded man—gradually—that he is closely related to other animals. At the same time it undercut the authority of religion for many people. In retrospect it appears that man resisted admitting fully his animal origin for a hundred years and that his final capitulation devastated him as much as he had feared that it would.

The behavioral sciences then added insult to injury. Psychologists have given man the impression that he responds like a laboratory rat to sensations and hormones and memories; the psychological terms used for his higher aspirations make them sound insubstantial or self-deceptive. Sociologists have made man think that his ethics and his deities, like his shelters, were fabricated by himself for purely utilitarian purposes.

An indirect cause for man's loss of self-respect may be the superhuman capabilities of his machines.

Perhaps another factor, in this pioneering country, is the lack of awe for the older generation and its values. In other parts of the world children are taught to feel respect for their parents and an allegiance to their parents' convictions. And the parents go on revering the grandparents. In America the father says, "Son, if you don't do better than I've done, I won't think much of you." This upside-down deference of the parent toward the child makes for geniality between the generations and for rapid innovation and material progress. But a youth develops merely an affectionate regard for his parent's character and a tolerance for his old-fashioned ideas. When he in turn becomes an adult, he looks for no particular respect—from his children or from himself.

The fact that the Victorian age set such exaggeratedly artificial, stuffy standards of propriety—in fact came close to denying sexuality and hostility altogether—may be another reason why succeeding generations have spurned dignity with such vehemence. Even words like "propriety" and "decorum" set our teeth on edge today.

So man's image of himself has been devalued and broken into a number of mechanical-seeming parts. It is one of his vulnerabilities that when he is called belittling names—like "animal" or "materialist"—he lowers his expectations of himself.

I believe that man's disillusionment is based on a fundamental misunderstanding of what his nature is. Of course he is closely related to other animals. But it is also true that he differs from them greatly. He is born with a nature that is potentially idealistic, spiritual, and creative.

These words are viewed so skeptically nowadays, not only because of the prevalent disenchantment but because of youth's suspiciousness about the older generation's hypocrisy, that I had better indicate what I mean by them: Idealism is to have faith in others and aspirations for oneself. The idealist reveres and cultivates courage, loyalty, generosity, perseverance, creativity. Idealism is what inspires a person to dedicate his life to the service of the community or to science or to creating an admirable family.

Man is a spiritual being in that—unless he is badly corrupted—he responds powerfully to nonmaterial stimuli: the beauty in nature or in art, the trust of children, the needs of helpless people, the death of a friend even though long absent.

Creativity refers not only to the fine arts—the designing of gardens and buildings, painting, sculpture, literature, music—but to inventions, scientific discoveries, engineering concepts. It may make an art of dress, manners, ceremonies, all of which give pleasure and inspiration as well as serve useful functions. They are, of course, the essence of civilization.

The Soul Is Made Out of Love for Parents

Young children (particularly between three and six) adore, are inspired by, and pattern themselves after their parents—not the parents as the neighbors see them, but glorified. They overestimate their parents' wisdom, power, and attractiveness. The boy yearns to be like his idealized father and other appealing males. He spends all day practicing, in activities and manner. This is how he matures emotionally and spiritually. He pretends to drive cars, go to the office or plant, mend things, preside at the family dinner table, with as much of the paternal style as he can muster. At the same time he develops an intense romantic attachment to his mother and idolizes her as his feminine ideal. As such she will strongly influence his choice of a wife when he grows up.

The girl between three and six years yearns to be like her mother—in activities, in manner, and in having babies of her own. She forms a romantic and possessive attachment to her father.

Because children are so very aware at this dependent age of how much their parents' love means to them, they are now inspired with a similar capacity to love generously their parents and other people. Out of this will eventually grow their devotion to their own children and their altruism toward humanity. Clinical experience shows that those unfortunate children who receive no love have none to give—ever.

There are several other developments in this three-to-six-year-old phase the significance of which in shaping later attitudes was discovered by Freud. These developments take place mainly at unconscious levels of the mind and do not sound plausible except to those who have studied children's thinking through psychoanalytic methods.

When boy and girl become aware, most often between two-and-a-half and three-and-a-half, that they are anatomically different they don't accept this as natural. The boy assumes that everyone was originally made with a penis as he was. Therefore he reasons that some injury must have happened to the girl. He goes on to the further assumption that if something bad could happen to her genitals, it could happen to his. Though this fear soon gets repressed, in the unconscious mind it continues to have a potent influence, especially in a boy's and a man's concern about the adequacy of his virility, both in the genital sense ("castration anxiety") and in the more general sense —as a competitor among males. Occasionally there is a boy who becomes so worried that he envies the girl for having nothing more to lose and would seriously prefer to exchange situations with her.

A little girl makes a similar misinterpretation, that she must have been deprived of a penis. But her reaction involves less anxiety about future harm, more resentment that her mother didn't love her enough to make her like a boy in the first place or that she caused some injury later.

This is also the age, between three and six, when interest in being married and having babies, and curiosity about sex are intense, even in the most properly brought up children. Little girls want to play at being mothers and boys at being fathers. They use a doll or a younger child for the role of baby. Little girls dream and talk, in our uninhibited country, about growing babies inside themselves. It's not as commonly realized that boys at three and four and five wish to perform exactly the same miracle of creation. If their mothers tell them that this is impossible, they will typically refuse to accept the reality for many months, insisting that they can do it if they want to. (This deep envy of the girl's creativity is the explanation of the custom in some parts of the world called "couvade": When a woman goes into labor and is taken to the labor hut to be attended by other women, her husband goes into labor too. He is taken to another hut where his men friends hold his hands and sympathize with him while he writhes in apparent pain.) As the little boy grows older he is forced gradually to face the reality that he cannot grow babies. But psychoanalysts have been convinced that his intense desire to do so fosters creativity in many of men's occupations, from the fine arts, science, and mechanics to making a shelf for the bathroom.

Sexuality Goes Underground

The boy's possessive love for his mother results in an increasing sense of antagonistic rivalry toward his father (whom he continues to love and admire at the same time) in the deeper levels of his feelings at about four, five, and six years. Playwrights and novelists have sensed this intuitively. (It is the theme of Sophocles' *Oedipus Rex.*) Freud documented it from his patients' unconscious minds and called it the "Oedipus complex." The boy fears, with childish logic, that his father is correspondingly resentful of him. This anxiety combines with his earlier worry about loss of the penis: He dreads—unconsciously—that his father may feel like injuring him genitally. (This is a frequent theme of bad dreams at five and six.) These anxieties build up to a very uncomfortable degree and eventually cause the boy to repress and deny his possessive love for his mother. His romantic attraction actually turns into an aversion, which mounts in intensity from about five to nine years of age. This is the "incest tabu"—against sexuality within the family—which is characteristic of all human societies, in varying forms, but does not occur in other species. It spreads and finally makes the boy leery of all members of the opposite sex. He squirms when his mother tries to kiss him, he groans at love stories on television and in movies, he makes a great point of scorning all girls. But most important of all, this temporary aversion to romance and sex, psychoanalysts believe, is what now makes him turn—with relief and special pleasure—toward impersonal, abstract, and symbolic interests, such as reading, writing, arithmetic, mechanics, science, nature. In other words, this is why children are emotionally ready for schoolwork at about six years. This is the emotional basis for intellectual curiosity. (These relationships, which do not seem plausible, become more evident during psychoanalysis. The patient's dreams may point clearly to the unconscious connections, for example, between curiosity about the origin of babies and the search for the solution of a scientific problem. To put it more generally, sexual interests can be sublimated into scientific and academic concerns.)

The boy's unconscious feeling of alienation from his father makes him look instead to heroes of history and fiction and the comics for his idols. It also makes him turn to teachers, to government officials, and to God as the highest sources of authority, displacing his father to a degree. It readies him, that is, for his religious life and for his law-abiding existence as a citizen.

Developments in the girl after five years are comparable but are different in their intensity. In the rivalry with her mother she does not feel nearly the degree of awe that the boy does for his father. (This is presumably in part because she is not as subjected to the fear of future injury as he.) Therefore she is not compelled to renounce so much of her physical affectionateness for her father or so much of her natural direct feelings for people in general. As a further consequence she is not as apt as a boy to become fascinated with such particularly abstract subjects as mathematics and, later, physics and law. Her deep confidence that she will bear children leaves her, in the average case, less preoccupied than the boy with trying to become a great artist, inventor, discoverer. There are probably inborn temperamental patterns in the girl as well as cultural pressures that contribute also to these differences.

The emotional development of man up to the age of five or six is not—except for his overidealization of his parents—basically different from that of the other higher animals. Like them he loves and depends on his parents, learns most of what he knows by imitating them. What distinguishes man so sharply from other creatures is the characteristics he acquires after five: the inhibition and sublimation of his sexual interests; his capacity for abstract thinking; his interest in symbols, systems, and rules; his inventiveness and creativity; his capacity for being inspired by heroes and spiritual ideals; his urge throughout history and throughout the world to define and worship a God. It is fascinating that these particularly constructive human characteristics are brought out in him by his having to relinquish his possessive yearning for one parent because of fear of and rivalry with the other.

This period of childhood, called latency because of the temporary suppression of sexual interests, is brought to an end by the glandular changes that introduce adolescence.

Rebellion Prepares the Way for Identity

The adolescent feels that his rebelliousness is simply a justified impatience with the bossiness of his parents. But the powerful motivating force at the unconscious level is his rivalry with the parent of the same sex. It is a recurrence of the rivalry of the four-and-five-year-old child but with greater vehemence now because of the full-size body and the full-blown aggressive and sexual instincts.

What compounds the adolescent's revolt is his own deep childhood dependence on his parents. This is much more difficult for him to throw off than the parents' actual control of him. (To escape the latter he would only have to leave home or go on a total strike.) However, pride would never let him admit this dependence even to himself; when he feels inadequate to stand on his own and meet new challenges, he is obliged to try to find a way to blame his parents for holding him back.

Adolescent rivalry and rebellion take obvious or obscure forms. A mountaineer's son who becomes angry at his father's domination may, without premeditation, knock him down and walk off to find a job. A boy brought up without respect for education or the law may displace his defiance of father onto the school authorities or the police. The son of a highly reasonable professional man may not be able to find any obvious paternal fault to justify his anger so he is reduced to picking on his mother or, at a deeper unconscious level, to failing inexplicably in his studies.

An exaggeratedly defiant girl may run away from home or carry on with men in a manner that shames and infuriates her parents.

Though rivalry is distressing in the way it strains family life at this age, it has vital functions to serve. It makes the young person want to leave home eventually and become fully independent. It provides the power behind his impatient drive to make changes in the world: to put an end to injustice, to introduce reforms, to discover new truths that supersede old concepts, to change the form of the arts. A surprising number of creative masterpieces and major advances in science have been achieved by young people just at the threshold of adulthood: the early music of Mozart, the early poetry of Keats, Newton's work with calculus, gravitation, and the light spectrum.

The young are not always right, any more or less than adults are. But when a situation is ripe for reform or change or advance, their automatic impatience with the way the older generation goes at things makes them at least a little more ready to see the new opportunities, less afraid to attempt to find new solutions.

The impatience of young people can make them deviate in any direction from the trend of the previous generation. This was brought home to me when I talked with a young woman who had worked since graduation from college at the slow, hard job of community organizing; she was helping poverty-stricken people to find ways to help themselves, primarily through political pressure at the municipal level. This type of social concern is so different from the preoccupation of college youths of a generation earlier who, according to their answers to questionnaires, were mainly interested in any job that paid the highest salary. The girl I spoke with had elected to spend her senior year at a university in the Soviet Union, partly drawn by reports from travelers of the enthusiasm of the Soviet people for building a socialist state and for absorbing all available forms of culture. But she found that many of the new crop of Russian students, though good companions, were impatient with discussions of the glories of socialism and seemed, on the surface at least, mainly interested in personal freedom and having a good time.

These examples made me realize that nothing can stay the same for long in any human society; that if a perfect society could miraculously be produced it would probably irritate the next generation. These examples show, in addition, that altruism and idealism are inner aspects of human beings that can come to the surface—or disappear—unexpectedly, depending no doubt on many factors; also that ideals can be taught by example and by good human relationships but they can't be preached into people beyond a certain point.

The ultimate problem of the adolescent and the young adult, as Erik Erikson has made clear in his books *Young Man Luther* and *Identity, Youth and Crisis*, W. W. Norton and Co., 1958 and 1968, is to find his identity, his sense of being a separate and independently functioning person. He may achieve this as early as his late teens, as late as his thirties or, in a rare case, never. When he has succeeded, he will know something about such specifics as what kind of occupation, friends, and place in the community he wants. But these factors are not the essence of identity; it is more basically an emotional state, a feeling of confidence about finally being one person, separate from others but able to make contact with them, and having some sense of direction. This state of mind can't be hurried. It seems to arrive when it's good and ready and no sooner.

Some youths appear to move without great strain or conflict from being their parents' child to being themselves. But quite a few—especially those who have come from closely knit families—show stress of any one of a dozen types.

In order to be sufficiently free to achieve his own identity a youth must largely outgrow his dependence on and emulation of his parents, who shaped his outlook and his personality from the time he was born. Yet during that long process he has made his parents a great part of himself. So in freeing himself from the parents within he has to pull himself apart. This is why it is painful—for him and for his parents.

Adolescents are often, without necessarily realizing it, experimenting with a variety of roles—man-of-the-world, roughneck, cynic, life-of-the-party, idealist—to see what feels right. They also use each other for discovering themselves: A lot of the endless conversation between pals is made up of delighted discoveries that their likes and hates are similar.

It is frightening for an adolescent (as it would be for an adult) to feel that he has no real identity; so, as he tries to shuck off the parentlike aspects of himself, he clings more closely to his friends and may pattern himself slavishly after them. One of the reasons he may act ashamed of his parents is the fear that if they stand out in any way it might interfere with his own acceptance by his group of friends, a matter that often seems of desperate importance.

Many adolescents at this stage make a wholesome religious affiliation on the basis of a need they feel for a personal relationship to God. A few individuals, panicky about their failure to find themselves, become obsessed with religion or mysticism.

Young people, if they have any spunk, have an impulse to avoid compromise and a middle course, in part because they so often feel that their parents have been corrupted by compromise. To be a purist seems more admirable; it also provokes the most arguments with parents and friends, which give the young person a certain grim pleasure and are also a means for testing out his ideas.

A youth with aspirations is on the lookout for hypocrisy in his parents. He would like to shed their standards, in order to be free to select his own; but ordinarily his conscience won't let him. If he can find his parents not living up to their own rules then he won't have to take them so seriously. A part of the cynicism that a youth so readily acquires may be sincere, resulting from the discovery that his parents and other respected people are not all that he imagined. But another part he pretends or greatly exaggerates in order to try to make his parents feel guilty—and to free himself.

For a few years while a young person is trying to find himself, society grants him a delay in settling down, what Erik Erikson calls a moratorium. He may shift jobs often or feel for a while no motivation to seek any job at all. Our particular civilization makes available, for those who have the brains and money, an almost limitless opportunity for more schooling, which can provide a respectable cover for uncertainty. But in another sense this only makes possible a greater prolongation of the inner distress. In the case of some students the identity conflict pursues them into the classroom and paralyzes their ability to learn or to write papers or take examinations.

Quite a few young people get stuck for a long time at a halfway point. They feel more and more strongly that they must differ from their parents. Yet they don't appear to come any closer to finding themselves. A common example is the boy who, the family hopes, will follow in his father's career. He has no idea what he'd like to do, he's only sure he doesn't want to do anything like what his father does. After several years, a negative resolve like this may suddenly disappear when the young man matures enough not to be afraid to compete with his father. (The shift often comes about halfway through college.)

More disturbing to the family are the youths who become nonconformist in appearance or behavior. (I don't include radicalism as nonconformity in this discussion.) Some of these individuals are functioning efficiently as students, or in untraditional jobs, and making good progress in finding themselves. Their appearance is only a declaration of independence, which is important to them now but will become less so as their achievements mount.

Others turn their backs on the whole contemporary scene. Some of these seek a better alternative based on group living, independence of material things, rejection of striving, the cultivation of serenity. These aims are somewhat similar to those of the early Christian communities.

It is important for conformists to realize that, generally

speaking, the nonconformist is not a lax person, quite the opposite. His high motivation and effectiveness will be evident when his identity crisis has been solved, whether or not he becomes more conventional. When a young person appears apathetic it is almost never apathy. He may be on dead center between opposing pulls. He may be suffering from depression or some other mental disturbance.

Inhibition in Childhood Fosters Idealism in Youth

The first tide of sexuality is awkward for beginning adolescents. The glandular drive is strong and comes on abruptly. It cannot quickly be integrated with tender, generous feelings.

The adolescent may first respond to his heightened feeling for people and get around the long tabu against the opposite sex by developing a crush on an admired person of his own sex. Later he can dream about advances to a far away actress, without fear of rejection or awkwardness. The next stage usually consists of falling earnestly in love with a succession of neighborhood girls whose appeal may be quite inexplicable.

The eagerness to love, the overestimation of the beloved, the reading-in of qualities desperately desired but not necessarily there, starts each attachment at a hectic level. Then if the beloved's personality turns out to be quite different from what the lover imagined, the affair soon cools.

Whenever a human being faces a new stage of development that requires a new capability (physical, social, or emotional), he feels a compulsion to keep practicing it, even at times when there is no particular use for it, until he not only masters the ability itself but integrates it into a usable place in his life. (For example, an infant keeps trying to stand up for months before he learns how to do this; then he insists on standing all day for several months, even when exhausted. Finally comes the stage when he stands when he needs to stand but can otherwise sit down.) At the same time that an adolescent is in love with one person he may feel a compulsion to test out his courage and charm and skill by trying to make advances to (or, in the case of a girl, inviting advances from) other members of the opposite sex, in a rather promiscuous spirit.

Though the pressure of the physical aspect of sexuality is intense in adolescence, part of it is still held in check and transformed into idealistic channels, to the degree that the family has aspirations. In such families the little boy's romantic adoration of his mother, suppressed for years, veiled, disembodied, now lends depth, mystery, and spirituality to his awakening love for a girl his age. He may be reluctant at first to recognize sexual feelings toward girls, especially those for whom he feels tenderness and respect. Even though this tabu lessens with time, he will retain a chivalrous attitude toward appropriate girls. He will want to protect them, please them, put them on pedestals, accomplish great things for them. Some of this attitude will persist throughout adulthood.

This idealization of women is a source of further inspiration to men. It combines with their drive to create;

and these two forces are the principal sources of men's poetry, novels, plays, music, painting, sculpture, much of which has had women as its subject. (The classic example is Dante's lifelong inspiration from his devotion to Beatrice, a young woman he had only seen, never known.) In a more subtle way these interwoven drives supply a part of the motivation to design buildings and bridges and machines, to pursue the sciences, to make technical advances. The biographies of a number of remarkably creative men show that as boys they were inspired to an unusual degree by the character of their mothers and by the fantasies, ambitions and ideals their mothers kindled in them.

The girl in adolescence goes through comparable romantic stages. Typically she doesn't have such a barrier of tabus to surmount, and she becomes more visibly preoccupied with boys at an earlier age. Psychoanalysis has shown that as she gradually becomes more realistic about the boys with whom she falls in love, the model set by her early-childhood devotion to her father plays an important though unconscious part. She daydreams about an idealized marriage and motherhood, and/or a career.

A family's level of aspirations affects the degree of inhibition and sublimation of sexuality. The Kinsey reports of a generation ago contrasted the differences of sexual behavior in people of various levels of educational attainment, from elementary school only, to graduate school. (The Kinsey families with higher educational levels are, to a degree, the same as those I refer to as setting high standards of behavior or high aspirations for their children. There are exceptions to this equivalence, of course: Parents of limited schooling may have very high educational and occupational aspirations for their child—and vice versa.)

One of the basic conclusions of the Kinsey reports was that in families at the lower educational levels the adolescent children are, on the average, less sexually inhibited and tend to come to intercourse at a relatively early age. Conversely the higher the educational level, the longer the postponement of intercourse and the greater the likelihood that it will not occur until engagement or marriage.

Another piece of confirmatory evidence in the Kinsey reports concerns the individuals who come from families of relatively low educational level but who are destined to move upward to a marked degree in their own educations and careers—because of unusual capability and ambition. In adolescence, before they have lifted themselves by their bootstraps, they already show the inhibition and delay in coming to full sexual experience that is characteristic of the levels to which they will eventually climb. The psychological presumption in such a case is that a boy had a specially close spiritual relationship with a mother who inculcated in him unusually high aspirations, along with relatively strong sexual tabus.

The inhibition and sublimation of sexuality referred to in this discussion do not mean that in adolescence there will be any less *interest* in romance and sex or that in eventual sexual relations there will be any less excitement or pleasure. The contrary is true. The Kinsey reports showed that in individuals at the lower educational levels (in whom there is the least sexual inhibition in adolescence) adult sexuality tends to consist of intercourse relatively abruptly initiated and relatively quickly over. (William Faulkner in a story once referred to it as a stallion's charge.) Whereas with progressively higher levels of schooling and aspiration there is usually (in adulthood) a prolongation and exploitation of the pleasures preliminary to intercourse, as well as of intercourse itself.

The Enrichment of Marriage

Falling in love in our Western civilization brings into sharp focus the idealistic and irrational aspects of romantic love. The lover (let's assume he is male for the moment) may become a changed personality. Attributes that he had previously claimed would be essential in a wife may be lacking in his beloved. She may even have traits which he found obnoxious in other girls. He greatly exaggerates her virtues and charms, ignores her faults.

In the process of psychoanalysis an individual may discover marked similarities between qualities of his beloved and of his parent of the opposite sex. To a degree falling in love is the same kind of romantic adoration that the small child had for his parent, now reactivated after many years of tabu and repression. This similarity helps to explain the suddenness, the intensity, the irrationality, the mysteriousness of the process, and why the lover feels the conviction that he has at last found the long-sought, the one and only person.

During courtship a man or woman will do anything in his power to please the beloved. What happens to this exuberant drive in marriage? In an ideal match it persists, at a less feverish level, for the rest of life. Husband and wife are buoyed up by each other's affection, support, and admiration; they achieve increasing thoughtfulness toward each other and skill in caring for each other. They succeed, in other words, in making a reality out of the overidealization of marriage each saw in early childhood.

Successful marriage is an art that can only be learned with difficulty. But it gives pride and satisfaction, like any other expertness that is hard won. It will also be an inspiration to the couple's children and friends. I would say that the surest measures of a man's or woman's maturity is the harmony, style, joy, dignity he creates in his marriage, and the pleasure and inspiration he provides for his spouse. An immature person may achieve great success in a career but never in marriage.

Idealism and Spirituality, a Summing-Up

Man's idealism, springing from his ambition to be like one of the parents he glorified in childhood and to be romantically worthy of the other, is part of the motivation of all his accomplishments—in improving and beautifying his home, writing a brief, composing a symphony, making love. And when an individual is idealized by others he is inspired to rise to their expectation. This is the effect of a group's faith in a leader, a husband's overestimation of the beauty and expertness of his wife, a wife's pride in her husband's minor success. This web of idealizations sustains the whole community and at times moves it forward.

The spirituality of man is derived from the joyous love he developed in early childhood for both parents, which then spreads to include other human beings, heroes, God, the beauty of art and nature.

So most of the beauty and progress man has contributed to civilization and the nobility he has achieved in his relationships with his fellow beings have sprung from his trusting, ingenuous idealization of his parents.

To summarize this more briefly still, man can build a reality in adulthood—sometimes a magnificent reality—out of what was partly an illusion in early childhood. This is the extraordinary power of our species.

These capacities are latent in every young child. But he will maintain high aspirations through childhood and into adulthood only if his parents foster them, in part by setting an example. If the parents live merely at the level of their bodily needs, even though law-abidingly, the child's overestimation of them will gradually shrink down, over the years, to life-size and provide him with little inspiration to go beyond that level. In the six-to-twelve-year-old period he will have only a limited interest in schooling, projects, science, heroic tales. In adolescence he'll be unconcerned with ideas or building a future.

By this gross oversimplification I don't mean to overemphasize the extremes or imply that there are merely two human patterns and that only one is worthy. In actuality there is every degree of these attributes and a countless variety of configurations and combinations. There are partners and places in the world for almost every type. I also don't mean that all standards and aspirations are worthy. Groups and families in various societies have jacked themselves up to high levels of stuffiness in manners or occupational aims, aversion to sexuality, pharisa-ism in religion, hypocrisy in moral standards which, far from enriching life, have withered or embittered it.

Though we can make an infinite variety of adaptations, there are pursuits and conditions of life that for most of us provide higher levels of satisfaction.

We feel happier when we are a part of some larger group to which we owe a major obligation—nation, church, business organization, extended family, or im-mediate family. This happiness begins back in childhood with our pride in being part of a family. It helps to explain why people are more friendly, less given to de-pression and suicide during wartime, when they feel im-portant to their country's cause and more closely tied to one another.

We feel more worthy and warmhearted when we are thinking of others, working for others. This comes from our early identification with parents who serve each other and their children. This is what holds societies together despite our species' greed, jealousy, and hostility.

We feel most inspired when on a project that challenges our highest capabilities. This is because we are creatures who from infancy strive for, gain enormous gratification from, and mature through the mastery of skills, the solu-tions of problems, the completion of jobs.

To balance this topic I should list some pursuits that tend to harden people's hearts, make them rivalrous and drive them apart. The best known are the strivings for wealth, power, and social position. I'll add one more, the acquiring of an exaggeratedly intellectual personality.

Belief in God and Belief in Man

The foregoing developmental view of man's nature seems to me compatible with Christianity and Judaism though it does not depend on any specific religious concept.

In the Western world the child under six accepts God on his parents' say-so—whether stern or benign—like a faraway grandfather. When he is between six and twelve, trying to outgrow some of his slavish admiration for his father, looking to the outside world for his standards, he takes readily to the idea of God as the highest authority. In adolescence, when he is searching for the meaning of his existence, he may reach out in a personal way to God. Or, as he attempts to free himself from his parents, he may rebel against their God—for life or for a few years.

A majority of human beings throughout the ages have believed in a god, though their concept of him has changed as they have changed their concepts of the world and of themselves. Compare the jealous, vengeful Jehovah of the Old Testament with the God of Love about whom Christ preached. Man's recent knowledge of biology, the atom, and the universe has made the man-shaped God of his forefathers less plausible. But it has not eradicated the emotional yearning.

Between a precise faith in God as revealed by a specific church and a bleak agnosticism, I think there is room for various religious, humanistic, and philosophical positions based on an understanding of man, which do not necessarily deny God the Creator though they acknowledge the difficulty of defining His nature. To the strongly or traditionally religious person such a belief in man might add nothing. But to a person with no specific religion (like myself) it may offer a reassuring or even inspiring credo. For it can integrate for him the animalistic, idealistic, and spiritual aspects of his nature, permitting him to respond to all these with a minimum of conflict. Even if he has no religion he may be moved by religious ceremonies because they speak with the poetry and dignity of past ages about men's aspirations to be worthy.

II
Problems of Sex
and Sex Role

The first six sections of this part discuss the question of why today's women are acting more and more like men and why men are entering women's activities, as if neither sex is satisfied with its lot. Some observers see this trend to sameness as welcome progress, believing that past distinctions in gender roles were arbitrarily imposed by men. I take the opposite view, that men and women are quite different in temperament and needs and that the feminists' effort to deny this is increasing the rivalry between the sexes and impairing the pleasure of both—but particularly of women. I, who have been considered a friend by mothers, worry about how many I will anger by taking this position.

The section called "Marital Problems That Begin in Childhood" is not so much a philosophical or clinical discussion as a simple listing of several of the irrational disturbances of marriage, included principally to add credibility to the Freudian concepts of sex and romance which are the underpinnings of Parts I and II.

The final three sections deal with aspects of the so-called sexual revolution: The first is the tendency of American adolescents, when experimenting with sexuality, to depersonalize it, to strip it of spiritual meaning. The second deals with the question of whether celibacy is now abnormal, or at least outmoded, as many young people assume. The third gives my relatively reactionary views on obscenity.

The Sexes Are Really Different

You can't tell whether there are innate temperamental differences between the sexes by determining what is the typical or normal role for man or for woman. Man has been a cruel warrior, a lace-trimmed dandy, a monk, a scientist. Woman has been a plodding farmer, a dancing girl, a novelist, even a bullfighter in ancient Crete. There are tribes where the only thing that the men do is to trade shells or carve gourds, while the women carry out all the jobs that keep body and soul together. And there have been societies in which a man rich enough to have servants could afford a wife who was only an ornament.

I realize that the question of innate differences is a highly controversial one and that some experts deny there is any such thing. What follows are my own observations of differences that I believe are at least partly innate though they may be accentuated or obscured by culture and family upbringing.

Very few girls right from birth seem to have as much striving and restlessness as the average boy. Even at one year of age I think boys have a greater interest in mechanical objects that can be investigated and manipulated. Girls as toddlers are more compliant than boys; they can be toilet trained more easily. More girls get high grades in school and college, because they are inclined to accept the instructor's word as long as it is reasonable.

31

Boys have a tendency to balk and argue, openly or
silently, which often keeps them from even hearing what
the instructor is saying. Women on the average are more
ready to make the multiple adjustments of marriage. With
eyes wide open they will overlook the imperfections and
absurdities of their husbands, provided their husbands
love and need them. A considerable majority of women
when they marry join the same political party as their
husbands; this doesn't mean that they have any less
capacity for analysis or opinion but that their devotion to
their husbands disposes them to see their husbands' point
of view.

Women are usually more patient in working at unexcit-
ing, repetitive tasks. Women working at a soda fountain
simply make sandwiches and drinks. Men must turn such
an occupation into a system, a combination of game,
ballet, and race against time in which they grab the
bread, slap on the filling, slice, and sling the sandwich—
all in one rapid, sleight-of-hand movement—meanwhile
bellowing cryptic orders back and forth and slipping
exaggerated compliments to their female customers.

Women on the average have more passivity in the
inborn core of their personality, though this can be
counteracted and hidden from view when they are
brought up in an atmosphere that encourages aggressiveness. The pattern of women's greater instinctive passivity
is evident in sexual relations. Girls and women who are up
against male indifference can be boldly provocative, as in
the case of fourteen- and fifteen-year-old girls who will
pursue the bashful boys of this age but quiet down if and
when older, more masterful boys become interested.
Women involved with men who clam up or are meek will

sometimes get wildly provocative with taunts, to make them angry and aggressive. But these kinds of provocation are to serve a passive need.

Boys and men have potentially much more aggressiveness, though this can be thoroughly controlled and curbed by upbringing. Even at two or three years they sense the general spirit of pistol play, long before they have any knowledge of death or ballistics. They continue to play cowboy or soldier with sparkling eyes and barking guns until they are nearly adolescent, an occupation that very few girls can be drawn into even briefly.

Young girls at an ice rink skate sociably with each other or practice twirls before the mirror. Boys of this age persistently and illegally skate against the current and play tag in and out amongst the nervous adults, enjoying the combat with each other and the indignation of the older people.

Erik Erikson in a revealing experiment presented small dolls representing adults and children, dolls' furniture, toy cars, building blocks to a series of American school-age boys and girls. He asked each one to set the stage and indicate a scenario for a movie about an exciting occurrence. Boys built towering structures with the blocks—a characteristic assertion of manliness—and then usually depicted a scene of violence, most commonly a burglary or a traffic accident. Policemen were used frequently, to arrest the culprit of a burglary or collision. Boys are preoccupied with aggression but equally with the need to control it.

Girls would use the blocks, if at all, to outline the rooms in a house. They would arrange the furniture by rooms. Then they placed members of the family in conventional domestic situations. A typical drama consisted of the two parents sitting in the living room listening while their daughter played the piano for them!

I suppose that if the girl had been reminded again, toward the end of her stage-setting, that the theme was to be an exciting event, she would have been able to substitute something more dramatic than piano-playing. But the significant thing was, I think, that by the time she had created the household plan she had forgotten that the drama was meant to be exciting and simply followed her temperamental inclination.

The emotional strengths that women contribute to family life in our society are realism, sensibleness, personalness. They sense clearly the human relationships around them. They have a strong urge to satisfy human needs. They enjoy making people comfortable. They sympathize with those who are suffering. (Suffering people make quite a few men acutely uncomfortable and impatient.) These qualities make women indispensable as wives, mothers, nurses, secretaries.

Women are not fascinated with gadgets for their own sake; they view them skeptically until they prove their utility. They see a car as simply transportation; they have no craving to buy a particular one because it is new-fangled or powerful; they generally object to the foolishness of spending extra money for such qualities.

There are aspects of these womanly virtues that bother men. When a case in the courts is settled in a way that accords with legal logic but happens to be unfair as applied in a specific case, a woman cries out impatiently, "How absurd!" Her husband says, "Don't you see that the law *has* to take this position, even if it occasionally causes injustice?" Helen Hokinson, the cartoonist, made gentle fun of plump, overly-personal older women. When a new president of the New York Central Railroad, years ago, decreed better food in the dining cars, Miss Hokinson had a matron exclaim cordially to the uncomprehending waiter, "I suppose we have your president to thank for this delicious *ragout.*"

The most valuable quality that men contribute to their family or organization or community is their ability to analyze a problem—to focus on one particular aspect of it, work out the theory behind it, find some kind of general solution. This is how they become, more often than women, inventors, discoverers, builders. More easily than women they can shut out the wholeness and the human realities of a situation in order to define an underlying abstraction. The disadvantage of this ability, for family life, is the tendency of many men to be somewhat absent-minded and impersonal. Girls can also be made impersonal but it takes much more mental disciplining by sternly intellectual parents and teachers to suppress their feelings.

One of the sharpest differences between the sexes, though a minor one, is woman's readiness to change her mind—for example, after ordering a meal and then hearing her friend order something else—and man's stubborn refusal to do so. A man feels that to be so fickle would imply that there was no judgment, no weight in his original decision. And he doesn't want to appear to be a follower of someone else.

In the same category but infinitely more dangerous is man's fear of losing face and his reluctance to admit publicly that he has made a mistake. (Societies and individuals differ a lot in this regard.) Families have been ruined and nations have been dragged through frightful wars to save men th•ᵤe discomforts.

When men can't establish an aura of authoritativeness by legitimate means they may try to do it with pomposity. (They do this less often now in the United States because pomposity is made fun of here.) The fear of not being accorded authority must have a lot to do with men marrying women two or three years their juniors, all over the world.

In many societies boys are taught that it is shameful to cry, to appear weak, to act fearful, or perhaps even to show feelings of any kind. There may also be an inborn factor in these attitudes. In any case it becomes a powerful motivating force, particularly in certain cultures. When men try to conceal their fearfulness with boldness they often get into trouble. Shame about showing feelings sometimes makes a man so insensitive to all the feelings of other people, as well as his own, that he is very difficult for family, friends, coworkers to live with.

Related to the fear of seeming weak is the impulse to court danger. There's a psychological mechanism called libidinization of pain: When a person, particularly in childhood, is subjected to an emotionally painful situation over a period of years, he comes to get a perverse kind of pleasure from it. Without conscious realization, he seeks to repeat it thereafter. A boy forces himself repeatedly to face danger in order to prove to himself and to the world that he is not afraid. At first this is almost as painful to him as it would be to a girl. But as the months and years pass he receives a pleasurable excitement from it. (I suspect that there is also an inborn factor in this male readiness to take risks.)

The compulsion to confront danger is one of the sharpest differentiations between the sexes. When a child falls through the ice from venturing out where he was forbidden to go, it is practically always a boy. When a child is caught halfway up a cliff, unable to climb up or down, it's always a boy. It's men who keep attempting the Himalayas. A great majority of women see danger simply and realistically as something to be avoided; only a few have been taught to enjoy it.

Men's readiness to take chances to prove their courage, which sometimes drives their wives to distraction, does have value. It is of course one of the main sources of the boldness with which they circumvent difficulties, defy traditions, change jobs, endure hardship. In the evolution of our species it made possible the hunter and the warrior.

Another aspect of the fear of weakness is the reluctance to ask for help. In psychiatry it's called "fear of dependency." A man driving a car in the country is obviously lost. His wife says, "There's a farmer; let's ask him the way." The husband brushes this suggestion aside, "I'm pretty sure the road I'm looking for is just ahead." Twenty minutes later they are still lost, the wife makes the same suggestion and the husband makes the same reply.

The fear of being effeminate or homosexual is another subdivision. European observers have been struck by how particularly strong this dread is in America. I remember during World War II the harsh punishment dealt out by the Navy to those caught in homosexual activity even when on liberty (the Shore Patrol spied to find it). I think of the promptness with which student councils of boarding schools and colleges have sometimes expelled students merely accused of it. The psychiatrist can explain that such fears are conscious or unconscious recognition of inner tendencies to effeminacy or homosexuality. But this tells little because all men are believed to have some degree of both; and a burly athlete may show more intolerance than a gentle scholar. So we end up saying only that some men are much more rigid, perfectionistic, and insecure about their virility than others.

Women often criticize men or laugh at them for being cowards because they meekly bow to customs and obligations of questionable validity. Many a man when uncertain whether to tip would much rather tip than not. He would rather tip too much than run the risk of tipping too little. A similar situation galling to wives is the contributions men are asked to make at their places of work—to charities, to testimonials, to political candidacies. This is partly a matter of submissiveness; I suspect that there are more men who are afraid of angering other men—particularly those in authority such as the boss, the policeman, the judge—than there are women in awe of other women— the woman boss, the school principal, the social leader of the community. (Few adults of either sex are scared of people of the opposite sex.) One underlying cause, in the unconscious, is that males assume in early childhood that they have a lot to fear from their fathers, while most girls assume they have little further to fear from their mothers.

Men also bow to custom because they are afraid of being thought inexperienced, innocent.

More significant than straight timidity is the sense of obligation of the well-disciplined male. This is the other side of the coin of his aggressiveness. Though he is by nature more aggressive, he is also designed to accept the curbing of his aggressiveness. More exactly, his aggressiveness can be turned inside out and becomes his law-abidingness. This disciplining takes place to the extent that he is raised in a society and in a family that is concerned with the civilizing of aggressiveness. There have been tribes in which the males preyed fiercely on other tribes, fought with fellow tribesmen, bullied their women. Even in our own kind of civilization there are neighborhoods (shrinking now) where men brawl frequently and have no respect for the law or women. At the opposite extreme (leaving out the effeminate man, who is a special case) might be the kind of scientist, for example, in whom no aggressiveness whatsoever is detectable. He is steered around at home by his wife. He is unassertive and considerate in his dealings with men. He would have a horror of breaking any law or regulation. Perhaps he has spent his life attempting to define further the laws of nature.

A good example of the conversion of aggression into cooperation occurs in automobile driving. There are men who criticize women for being terrible drivers. They can't be referring to the statistics on accidents or deaths because these show that the dangerous drivers are mainly men, asserting their hostile competitiveness and their virility in a perilous manner. The critical males are referring, for instance, to the woman driver who doesn't think to get into the left lane before making a left turn or the right lane for a right turn. The kind of man who is always in the correct lane is there because his inborn aggression, inverted into cooperativeness by strict parental training, is constantly reminding him to be considerate. Many a man in the wrong lane is there because his aggressiveness was never well curbed. The woman in the wrong lane is rarely a ruthless or even an inconsiderate person; her nonautomotive life shows this. There is simply not enough hostility in her make-up to worry her conscience.

A core problem for men, of course, is the question of the adequacy of their virility. This is a matter of only barely perceptible uncertainty for some, an incessant preoccupation—conscious or unconscious—for others. Fear of sexual impotence is its most obvious aspect; this is an ingredient of a large proportion of all jibes and dirty stories, a cause of marital distress—more often to husbands than to their wives—a common cause of infidelity on the part of men trying to prove themselves to themselves.

The striving to prove virility plays a part in competition with other men for jobs, money, fame, athletic laurels, women; in the size and power of automobiles; in the inclination to boast and strut and declaim. It is demonstrated more convincingly when men stand up to each other in bargaining and fights.

Its early root is the small boy's increasing awareness of and resentment about his father's impressive genital head start. This phallic focus of rivalry becomes a part of the boy's competitiveness with other boys; it shows up in frequent locker room kidding about the smallness or largeness of different boys' genitals and in competition for distance in urinating.

Each male's concern about his virility continues throughout boyhood and manhood and is affected by all the other vicissitudes of his life. His assurance is increased by any kind of material success, or honors, by the depth of his wife's pride and appreciation, by the respect of men and women generally, as well as by his genital potency. Of course most men limit the risk of failure by carefully trimming their ambitions to their capabilities. But there is always a minority of daredevils, some of whom succeed remarkably because of their brazenness.

The innate differences between the sexes have been built into our species during the long course of evolution by the process of natural selection. That is to say, they contributed to a successful family life, one which kept the father and mother in a harmonious, stable relationship so that they could divide the jobs in an efficient way, fend off threats, human and otherwise, safeguard and raise children trained to take over in their turn. Man has been the fighter, protector, theorizer, inventor. Woman has been empathizer, comforter, realist, preserver.

When husband and wife have distinctive roles to play, each is likely to be more valuable and pleasing to the other—and also more proud of his own contribution. A woman is glad to have a husband who will take over the unpleasant disagreement that has cropped up between her and a tradesman or landlord. When she is emotionally upset, her husband's emotional self-control is usually a support (as long as he is not the person she is angry with). A man who can fix the plumbing or a doorbell will be more impressive to his wife (and to himself) if she is relatively helpless in such fields. She will be more appreciated as a fine cook if he is not.

Occasionally a couple will say they live particularly harmoniously because of being in the same field—the husband and wife for instance who are both physicians and enjoy discussing their common professional concerns.

But for most couples to be in the same field of activity introduces an element of competition that puts extra strains on the marriage. In stage and screen marriages, for example, both partners are competing for popularity, critical acclaim, salary. I've been told by several women how hard it is to have a husband who is a genius in the kitchen or who seems much more successful in managing or eliciting the affection of the children. When a husband tells his wife about his troubles at the office he wants her to sympathize with him in his feelings of frustration. He does not want her to tell him how easily she herself would have surmounted these difficulties.

Women's Rivalry with Men

The little girl's envy of the boy's penis and the boy's envy of the little girl's ability to grow babies create rivalries that persist into adulthood. These are exaggerated in certain societies and families, minimized in others. The bossy, competitive woman is common in literature and life. Way back in the fourteenth century the Wyfe of Bath, in Chaucer's *Canterbury Tales,* explained frankly that what women want most in the world is domination over their men.

In simple societies that have depended on male strength and aggressiveness men have more often been domineering. As they have built civilizations based on mental skills, records, the arts, they have been inclined or persuaded to give increasing respect to women. Nevertheless, up until modern times, men retained much greater authority for themselves in civil and religious law and deprived women of education, suffrage, legal and financial rights, even in Western civilization.

American women seem to me to have gone further than those in comparable societies in taking over the leadership in their families. One explanation sometimes offered is that men in a pioneering society, such as ours used to be, were so preoccupied with taming the wilderness that they left the children more exclusively to the women; mothers then became more influential than fathers as creators and transmitters of the culture and as bosses of the home. By contrast the men in settled societies are thought to take more time to preside over family councils and to get together with other citizens to decree the standards.

It's true in general that a subjugated group in a society becomes more rebellious and demanding *after* it has been granted some rights. So perhaps it was the increased authority that women gained in coming to the colonies that put them in a mood to demand more.

The feminist movement—for rights for women—had its roots in the philosophy of humanism and equalitarianism of the late eighteenth century, which contributed to the ideologies of the American and French revolutions. Feminism first reached full force in America, beginning in the mid-nineteenth century. Its leaders roused women to demand educational, occupational, legal, financial, and political equality—which they have since largely but not completely won. The women of other Western nations gradually followed suit, starting with those of the Protestant countries.

But I would say that psychologically the most vehement feminists were motivated not so much by altruism toward their own sex as by an unusually fierce envy of men. They not only demanded that women have the same rights, but insisted that they are essentially the same as men—in range of personality traits, in capabilities, in drives, in emotional needs, in what they have to contribute to society. In this claim to sameness they were mistaken, I think. They were also mistaken in assuming that everything men have or do is desirable.

Gradually the view that women are essentially the same as men has been accepted by an ever larger proportion of American women, without their stopping to realize what a revolutionary concept it is, or even being aware that people have not always thought this way. When I have lectured in universities and have referred to the differences between the sexes in temperaments and satisfactions, young women have come up afterwards to ask incredulously whether they heard me correctly.

The main harm from the assumption of sameness is that it encourages an exaggerated rivalry that, I think, impairs the happiness of both sexes and the harmony between them.

Feminism secured education for girls. Then the nature of the education that was provided for them served to reinforce the competitive type of feminism. The famous people held up for admiration and emulation were, of course, the successful statesmen, generals, explorers, scientists, inventors, industrialists, writers, artists, most of them men, celebrated for their occupational achievements, not for the happiness of their homes or the fine qualities with which they imbued their children. So the imagination and idealism and ambition of girls, like boys, have been channeled toward the traditional careers of men. They have assumed that if they wanted recognition from the world it would be by making a contribution outside the home. They have learned to enjoy the challenge of competing with men—just as men have always enjoyed it.

Research has shown that students pick up the basic attitudes of teachers through identification more than by precept. So those women instructors in girls' colleges and schools (unmarried and married) who have been scornful of domesticity and of men have thus had a special influence.

Girls have been expected to participate in the same sorts of extracurricular activities as boys, often including compulsory athletics, which a large proportion of them detest and some of which, I think, encourage the wrong kind of aggressiveness.

Women began making their way into various professions and into a few industries in the last part of the nineteenth century. It was the labor shortage of World War I that drew them in large numbers into many new fields. This helped to break down the prejudice of husbands who had previously felt that it was a reflection on their manly earning power if their wives worked. It was also during and after World War I that women began cutting off their long hair and wearing brassieres designed to flatten their breasts. By the 1930s, women college graduates in their letters to their class secretaries were apologizing if they had failed to develop a career, confessing that they had "only raised several children."

There has been an increasing trend—with temporary

reversals—for women to wear clothes and hair styles like men's. Many now walk stridingly and talk assertively. Some of them slap backs, shout, guffaw, drink, and tell dirty stories. I'm not referring here to the very occasional masculine woman who really feels like a man but to the everyday types who merely imitate and compete with men.

The proportion of women who are competitive with men is higher among those who have been to college, I believe, though I have no figures to prove this. I'm thinking not only about obvious rivalry in job preference and job performance. I'm thinking of the less visible differences that a man feels in talking socially or dealing occupationally with a woman who has the constant itch to argue and criticize, however subtly, and with a woman who accepts him comfortably as he is.

Today girls show a greater aggressiveness in sexual advances. This was brought out in the spontaneous comments of college students and faculty in several recent studies of sexual behavior: Girls themselves complain of how much sexual initiative they often have to take. Faculty people report their surprise at what a large proportion of the provocation and advances they happen to see is now initiated by girls. When recently I talked to an audience of college men on a different subject and referred casually to my impression that our culture is encouraging young women to be overly aggressive toward men, there was sudden vehement applause, much more than greeted anything else I said.

To some moderns this sexual boldness of girls seems like a wholesome change. They feel that men in past times asserted, without justification, a monopoly right to sexual initiative. This sounds plausible; but to me it ignores the temperamental differences between the sexes. I believe women are designed in their deepest instincts to get more pleasure out of life—not only sexually but socially, occupationally, maternally—when they are not aggressive. To put it another way I think that when women are encouraged to be competitive too many of them become disagreeable. I remember an article by a golf professional who expressed his consternation at the behavior of a third of the women who play the game at a typical club. They respond to the competition, he said, with conduct toward each other that ranges from arrogant to brazenly dishonest. It's not that men have nobler characters. It's that men are designed and reared to compete but also to keep their competitiveness disciplined within conventional bounds.

When a woman refrains from competing with men, or when a woman is gentle in manner, this doesn't mean that she has to be submissive. She has her sphere, her power, her expertness, her indispensability (if she's any good), her self-respect and the respect that she can demand from men. The person who thinks that to escape domination a woman must have 50 per cent equality—quantitatively and qualitatively—has fallen into the trap of thinking always in terms of competition, as if woman is always in a race with man and must be exactly even or ahead or ignominiously behind. I'd say that man and woman are meant to be on separate roads, however close, not racing; and that on the occasions when their roads might cross, one defers at one time, the other at another, depending on the practical and ceremonial requirements.

The Causes of Passivity and Domesticity in Men

As more women have become dominant, more men have become passive or have invaded what were considered women's spheres.

Whereas in most parts of the world the father is officially the senior authority to whom are referred the more serious family decisions, in this country in the twentieth century the mother is often the dominant figure, and in such families the father plays a secondary, more passive role. In many comic strips and television comedies the father is a stupid, bumbling, ridiculous figure. The pattern of male passivity occurs in other Western countries but not as frequently and not as obviously. The European woman with a dominating spirit is restrained by the conventions; and the man, however meek, is emboldened by this external support.

Quite a few American men who are successful in the world and who are not submissive at all in other relationships take an amused pride in referring to their wives as "The Boss." This doesn't mean that these men are necessarily dominated in fact by their wives; but it is significant of a twist in male attitude in America that they enjoy pretending that they are subordinates. Other American men call their wives "Mother." Of course there is at least a small element of son-mother relationship in all marriages (just as there is a daughter-father element), but in other countries this is not a matter for public announcement.

Men have been doing more of the marketing, cooking,

dishwashing, diaper changing, infant feeding, child tending. This has seemed fair enough, particularly in those families in which mothers have outside jobs and are as tired as their husbands when they come home. (On this theme of fairness I recall a magazine article by a woman who seriously advocated an exact fifty-fifty split in all home chores as the answer to the emotional problem of modern marriage. I suspect this would make matters worse. I know from pediatric experience that the parent who tries to allay rivalries between children by hairsplitting justice only accentuates the rivalry.)

What has lured men into fields previously considered women's? My belief is that men are reacting, unconsciously, to the success that women have achieved in most occupations previously considered men's. I mean that men no longer can take pride that only they have the strength, courage, skill or shrewdness to tackle the tough jobs of the world and bring home the bacon. Also, women used to emphasize their physical weakness, their timidity, their mechanical ineptitude, which allowed men to feel protective and ingenious. My point is that when men are deprived of the satisfaction of making distinctively masculine contributions they more readily respond to their latent envy of women and shift over toward women's traditional occupations. Not every man would feel threatened by a highly successful wife, but this is the kind of ego vulnerability that many, many males have. Similarly a woman deprived of traditional feminine gratifications is more apt to show envy of men.

I don't mean for a minute that every woman who takes a job or puts on a pair of slacks is trying to usurp man's place or that the man who barbecues the steaks or enjoys excursions with his children wants to replace his wife. There are many different influences that can lead to the same action, including practical necessity; and temporary styles and fads sweep people into activities they would not have entered on their own initiative alone. The motive, the attitude, is the significant criterion.

You might ask whether the kind of marriages that occur between dominating women and passive men aren't ideal for both. They can be. But the reason that many of them produce strain is because the individuals involved are only partially off kilter. The bossiness of a woman may persuade her to marry an ineffectual man; but there is another side of her that is realistically critical of his imperfections and would like a more inspiring mate. That is to say, there is usually a discrepancy within the off-kilter individual between his neurotic, unconscious desires and his more wholesome needs; and this discrepancy causes him to demand too much from his spouse and to give too little.

It is sad to see how neatly the tendencies toward female domination and male passivity may be passed from generation to generation—though not always, by any means. The examples I'll give are oversimplified, to clarify the main points.

The daughters of rivalrous women tend to identify with their mothers in being dominating. They readily compete with their brothers. Since their fathers are likely to be passive in certain respects, this quality in males acquires a romantic appeal for these girls, early in childhood, and may enter into their marriage choice in adulthood.

A boy is typically made passive by a mother who's highly rivalrous with men. She is particularly proud of producing a son. (The unconscious statement may be, "Though I can't be a man, I can create one.") But she's likely to make a point of teaching him to do housework and help with the baby. She tends to overmanage him, to usurp his initiative, to curb his particularly masculine aspirations and normal aggressiveness. He may grow up with an impaired confidence about his maleness, about his ability to compete enjoyably with other males. A boy normally acquires much of his manliness and effectiveness by identifying with a father well-endowed with these traits. But if, as often happens, a dominating woman is married to an unassertive man, their son may be let down by his father as much as he is held down by his mother. At the worst, he may turn out an ineffectual mother's boy. On the other hand, if things go right, he may eventually compensate with intense determination and productivity. The boy whose romantic ideal was set by devotion to a dominating mother may respond most in adolescence or adulthood to a girl with the same vigorous personality.

The greatest inaccuracy in this oversimplification is that all the children of such couples don't turn out to be replicas of their parents. They are born with different temperaments; they find their situations different depending especially on whether they are first, last, or middle child; and—most important of all—they evoke different aspects of their parents. A mother may be oppressively managerial with one son and be surprisingly tolerant of the independence of another.

Reluctance to Acknowledge the Opposite Sex

I've read articles by European women and men about their impressions of Americans as husbands and wives— usually not their own husbands and wives, by the way— and I've talked with several on the same subject. Though they are generally enthusiastic, they all mention the failure of many Americans to be appropriately attentive and engaging toward members of the opposite sex, whether they are husband and wife or merely casual acquaintances.

European women remark that American husbands are faithful, extraordinarily generous in terms of money and household equipment, devoted to their wives, and helpful with the children. But they often fail to give a European wife or woman acquaintance the feeling of being regarded and treated as an attractive woman. Many an American husband and wife behave in public, as if they were partners of the same sex in a business. The American at a dinner party may be friendly enough to the woman next to him, but he seems afraid to converse with her in any different manner than if she were a man.

These are not exclusively European comments. Similar complaints are sometimes made by women of the northeastern and southeastern states about some of the men from other regions of the United States. The American style of male bashfulness and romantic immaturity reaches the level of caricature in the typical cowboy story in which the hero is as scared of women as a nine-year-old boy would be.

European men generally agree that a remarkably large number of American women are beautiful; they make conscientious mothers and wives; they respond capably to challenges. But from a romantic point of view many of them are disappointingly self-sufficient and self-centered —as if they had no real need of men. This fits with the enthusiastic comments of American men who have lived in Europe or the Far East, about how extraordinarily attentive and personal the women in those regions are.

Americans can now talk boldly or jokingly about sex in mixed company—though I think there is often a forced quality to this. Americans are presumably as sexually competent in the bedroom as any other group. But what's under discussion here is something more subtle and apparently more difficult to attain: sufficient sexual and romantic maturity to allow a person—man or woman—to show, whenever he is dealing with a member of the opposite sex, that he is pleasantly aware of this and that he can be appropriately attentive and charming, without implying an intention of further seductiveness. The attentiveness that the Europeans speak of is milder than flirtatiousness. It is not a sexual advance but a sexual recognition.

This American sexual bashfulness is in part a result of the dominant mother pattern that I have been discussing. I think, too, that Puritanism is still making us Americans uneasy, even when we are going to extremes of sexual crudity in literature and drama and conversation in order to prove that we have overcome Puritanism at last.

Fulfillment and Jobs for Women

Among American mothers, especially those who've been
to college, there are many who complain of a chronic
malaise: They feel trapped by having to be with their
children all day, or they miss any sense of fulfillment in
their existence—or both. They think that going back to
work would be a solution.

They say they feel like idiots after talking to children
for eight hours; they say reproachfully to their husbands,
"You've been with interesting people all day." I myself
always thought children's conversation was a lot more
original than a majority of adults', who prefer to converse
in clichés. It's normal, though, to want to be with other
adults; but whereas in most simpler cultures a young
woman finally joins the circle of women she's been looking
forward to all her life when she has her child, in our
culture she's isolated in her home for the first time. Another cause of strain in our country is that, according to
popular American psychology, a mother must try to be
loving and understanding at all times; otherwise her child
will show the lack. That's an impossible obligation; it
takes a lot of the fun out of child care and replaces it with
guilt.

Fulfillment is probably increasingly elusive for women
because it comes from a sense of performing a difficult
and important function to the best of one's ability. The
electrical household aids, the ease of buying family neces-

sities during an era of prosperity, the small number of children in the average family, all make a mother feel less essential nowadays. Filling up her spare time with taxiing children and doing committee chores only fragments further her sense of purpose. I've heard women boasting that they can sleep late because their thoughtful husbands get their own breakfasts. This is a small example in itself and probably the wrong one for a man to bring up; but I would say that it's bad enough to convince your husband that you aren't essential, it's worse to convince yourself.

I believe that the basic reason behind the other reasons why mothers feel unfulfilled is because child-rearing in our artificial, competitive society carries no prestige. Many women who have attended college—like many men —acquire an academic snobbery according to which any knowledge that hasn't been learned in the university doesn't amount to much and any job that you can get without a degree has little dignity. This feeling is why they have a condescending opinion of the capabilities required in and the value to society of child-rearing. (Any girl above the age of thirteen, even a mental defective, can have a baby.) Such women feel that raising children has sentimental and family importance, of course, but that it cannot give career gratification. When the deeper instincts of such young women draw them into marriage and motherhood, they feel as if the door to the kinds of fulfillment they envisioned has been shut in their faces.

A group of medical students and I were discussing the boredom that some women feel with child-rearing. The only woman student in the group said that she would find it boring too. I asked her if child psychiatry would be boring, since it involves long hours of intense concentration with a series of difficult children each day. "Of course not," she answered. I asked, "Why not?" "Because," she said impatiently, "the psychiatrist is trying to accomplish something." The male students groaned at this unwitting insult to motherhood.

Why do men choose careers working with children in psychiatry, psychology, pediatrics, school teaching, social work? They find it fascinating and creative work to help children to develop well. In one sense they are trying to do mothers' work.

The subject of jobs for women is complex and controversial. A man who offers his opinion on it is asking for trouble, but I have to include mine in order to round out my theme.

I assume that the present trend of more and more women wanting to go to work will continue. They have every right to do so, as long as the children's emotional needs are thoughtfully met, especially in the preschool years. Women have lots of years for work nowadays since early marriages and family planning mean that, on the average, they will have their last child well started in elementary school by the time they are thirty-five years of age. (In earlier generations women had children right up into their forties and by the time the last one was in school they didn't have much ambition about starting to work. The housework took twice as long then, too.)

Women, I believe, should be able to get any kind of training they want and have an equal chance with men to get any jobs they want, at equal pay, including those jobs requiring a high degree of aggressiveness when that is their dish.

On the other hand I feel that since women have an inborn aptitude for—and naturally get gratification from —understanding and helping people and creating beauty, and since most of them are going to spend fifteen to twenty-five years of their lives primarily raising their children, it would be fairer to them if they were brought up at home and educated at school and college in such a spirit that they would enjoy, feel proud of, and be fascinated by child-rearing rather than frustrated by it. Then they would be less inclined to be rivalrous with their husbands and other men. If they sought outside jobs, they would prefer those that are compatible with feminine drives, for example, as nurses, social workers, teachers, librarians, designers and merchandizers of clothes, secretaries, physicians, psychologists, writers, actresses, architects, and decorators. And if they had careers in medicine or architecture, for instance, they should be able to make distinctly feminine contributions to the advancement of these fields, rather than compete with men in the usual manly traditions of these professions.

In bringing up our children—boys as well as girls—I think we should be enthusiastic about their maleness or femaleness as attributes to be proud of, enjoyed, emphasized, rather than taken for granted or even denied as they so often are today. A boy should know that his father enjoys his company in a special way because they can talk about cars or carpentry or sports. Even a small boy should feel that his mother appreciates his manly help in carrying things for her, opening doors, running errands, fixing things.

A girl needs from her father compliments on the attractiveness of her appearance, on her skill in feminine occupations, and particularly on her thoughtfulness and helpfulness.

Most of all a girl needs a mother who shows warm affection for her and who shows enthusiasm for playing the role of woman herself—with verve and style. It is in these matters that many American women depreciate womanhood, depreciate themselves, depreciate their daughters. They fail to inspire in them any conviction that the role of woman and mother can be as fascinating and creative as any other, whether or not there is an outside career.

In high school and college girls should be encouraged to take (in addition to various kinds of theoretical courses) practical courses that will foster their enjoyment of children—participating as teachers' assistants in a nursery school or acting as nurses aides on a children's hospital ward—which could be linked to theoretical courses in child development or human relations. (Men should take the same kinds of practical courses.)

Marital Problems That Begin in Childhood

That human sexuality—far from being the simple instinct that some people speak of today—is elaborately patterned in each individual by the particular relationships that developed between him and his two parents at various stages of childhood is shown dramatically by some of the irrational or even bizarre disturbances of marriage.

Tensions develop within every marriage, of course. One spouse persistently disappoints or angers the other—by failure to carry out his responsibilities, by offensive habits, by unfaithfulness. Whatever the original cause, when one partner temporarily loses the desire to please the other, the latter is apt to reciprocate. There is a descending spiral for a while. After a blowing off of resentment and an open or silent acknowledgment of fault, there is usually a readjustment on a somewhat different basis than before, usually more mature. In other cases there is insufficient maturity in one or both spouses to spur them to make the reparative effort. They may separate, or continue to live together in a state of hostility.

If both partners grew up in intensely wrangling families they may settle down into a pattern of regular battles so violent that the neighbors assume divorce is inevitable and imminent. Yet each fight may end in enthusiastic intercourse. After years of this alternation of war and peace it becomes apparent that this is the kind of relationship, called sadomasochistic, which both partners really enjoy and need.

The common disturbance in which a man or woman has an excessively dependent, demanding attitude toward the spouse, without expecting to give anything in return, is usually a reflection of his own child-parent relationship. This pattern proves to be more than most spouses can tolerate; the exception is the "sugar daddy" whose greatest pleasure comes from indulging endlessly a childish-seeming girl. There's an occasional wife, too, whose only desire is slavishly to indulge her husband.

The psychoanalyst sees highly specific disturbances in marriage that show the negative power of the Oedipal relationship. A man or woman may choose a spouse with a prominent trait that the world would call undesirable or worse but that, it turns out, is strongly appealing to this individual because, in a subtle unconscious way, it recalls a similar trait in the parent of the opposite sex. Such an individual may be able to fall seriously in love only with a curmudgeon, an alcoholic, a constant quarreler, or a pompous ass. The boy who grows up with a silly or aggressive or garrulous mother may respond strongly only to a girl from the same mold. A girl may need a husband who is as jealously possessive as her father. It's not that any of these patterns must or always will be carried over from childhood into marriage. But the fact that they are fairly frequently carried over is evidence of the power of the Oedipal attachment and an explanation of why such an intricately formed relationship as human marriage frequently shows flaws.

In many marriages there is a distinct letdown in attentiveness, in efforts to please, as soon as the wedding is over. Why should the long-sought bliss prove illusory so soon, for so many? In one case it is evidence that the strongest drive was not to achieve a grown-up love relationship but simply to win possession, as an envious child thinks he wants anything another child has but discards it as soon as he secures it. In another case the prompt outbreak of disagreeableness simply represents a carry-over into marriage of the chronic hostility of the original family, which was temporarily hidden during the wooing period.

When the infatuation that went to the beloved during

the courtship reemerges soon after the marriage as infatuation for a new person it may point to other aspects of Oedipal love. In childhood, of course, the possessive love of the parent was, in effect, forbidden. This forbidden aspect of love may, if it is too exaggerated, carry over as the most exciting element in an adult's romantic life. After marriage his romantic love of his spouse is not only not forbidden but is now obligatory; this requirement may be enough to detach most of the romance from his spouse and set it free to look for another forbidden attachment.

A second and more common factor in extramarital infatuation is an unconscious pleasure in making the spouse jealous. A boy who grows up with a very possessive mother senses how jealous she becomes whenever he shows an interest in a girl. This becomes, at the unconscious level, an integral and exciting part of his relationship not only to his mother but later to the girl he marries. So, making his wife jealous may not be a sign of weakening of the marriage but of its intensity, in a highly neurotic way. Both of the above explanations for infatuation outside marriage may pertain to women, too.

The problem of the man who is always trying to seduce a different woman may be his doubt at the unconscious level about his potency, irrespective of how good it is in fact. The woman whose behavior with all men is exaggeratedly seductive may harbor a deep uncertainty about her attractiveness. Seductiveness can also primarily express hostility to the opposite sex, left over from resentment toward a parent in childhood: Snare him and then drop him.

A few people avoid marriage permanently and substitute affairs. On the surface they fear that marriage will come to feel like a prison or that it will develop the same strains for them as it did for their parents. At unconscious levels they are apt to have more basic anxieties about their adequacy in one or another respect. This solution has great superficial appeal—all the excitement of secret, forbidden, romantic sexuality without family responsibility and family grubbiness. But these individuals have to cut themselves off from lifelong satisfactions that most people demand from marriage: the reliving of childhood and the achievement of a sort of immortality from rearing their own children, the participation as a family in the community, the ties to children and grandchildren in the last third of one's life when other gratifications peter out. Most alliances without children prove transitory.

Depersonalization of Sex in Adolescence

When an adolescent boy and girl are having a succession of dates or have agreed to go steady there is often, in America, a paucity of the signs of romantic love. By romantic I mean all the aspects of love beyond the purely physical attraction: the tenderness, the conviction that the beloved is uniquely attractive, the constant preoccupation with him or her, the desire slavishly to serve and please, the delight in every rediscovery that the beloved reciprocates, the wish of the couple to be always together, to share all thoughts and plans, a sense of optimism and omnipotence that, together, they can overcome all diffi-

culties, a heightened appreciation of all forms of beauty
and spirituality.

Instead there may be preoccupation with the physical
aspects of the relationship and at the same time a deper-
sonalization of it, as if it weren't a part of themselves. An
American student who had just returned from a post-
graduate year in a European university described to me
the contrast: European students who fall in love seem
enraptured by the beloved and by the state of being in
love, he said. Many Americans seem cool, analytical, or
exploitative. He recalled with distaste the tendency of
himself, his male friends, and their girls to spend a lot of
their dating hours discussing the pros and cons of various
stages of physical intimacy, as if the couple were taking
part in a university seminar on the physiology and psychology of sex.

A partial explanation, I suspect, is that we Americans
are living in a society and in a period when there are
unusually confusing contradictions in regard to sexuality.
There is Puritanism still, despite the revolt against it, and
the normal restraint of those raised with aspirations. On
the other hand there is the general weakening of religious
values and the reversion to "naturalness," the advocacy of
respected leaders and churchmen of an end to hypocrisy
and guilt about sex, the great uncertainty among parents
about what is true or right and their fear of disturbing
their children's social or sexual adjustment. So young
people feel they have permission to be "honest" and free.
Dating and bold biological talk begin at an unpreceden-
tedly young age, before there is much capacity to love.
Yet on theoretical grounds I believe that young people
brought up with aspirations must still feel at the uncon-

scious level the inner necessity to inhibit some aspects of their sexual-romantic drive.

The result, I think, has been a paradoxical reversal. In earlier generations aspiring adolescents fell very much in love in the romantic sense but were inhibited against recognizing or expressing physical desire in these relationships. In fact, at the turn of the century some of the most protectively brought up girls had no conscious awareness that there was such a thing as intercourse until they were married. Carefully reared boys and girls previously found physical outlet most often in masturbation, though it caused worry and guilt.

Now by contrast many adolescents permit themselves to go far in physical intimacy but unconsciously resist yielding to a tender, idealistic love for these same partners. So the common denominator, fifty years ago and today, is an inner need to keep physical sexuality and tender love separated.

It seems significant of the times that even Henry Miller protests that sexuality in the minds and behavior of many people has become a mechanical, loveless matter.

Is Celibacy Abnormal?

From talking with college psychiatrists I understand that the individual who most needs reassurance today is the boy or girl who has grown up with greater than average restraint, who is not ready for marriage or an affair, and who is therefore teasingly accused, by more experienced friends, of being impotent or frigid or otherwise abnormal. The references he hears from many sides about the sexual revolution reinforces this sense of peculiarity. Is celibacy abnormal now?

Closely allied is another question: Are Freud's concept that idealism and creativity are related to the inhibition and sublimation of sexuality and the Kinsey reports' statistical support for this concept valid any longer?

I'll summarize the conclusions I've come to from reading studies recently published and from group discussions in which I've participated, all involving college students.

A recent questionnaire survey by Vance Packard of juniors and seniors across the country indicates that 58 per cent of the men and 43 per cent of the women have had intercourse, compared to Kinsey's figures, of a generation ago, of 51 per cent and 27 per cent respectively, a slight change for the men, a significant change for the women.

Those of both sexes who have engaged in "everything but" intercourse find it difficult to explain why they draw a line here, since fear of pregnancy does not play nearly as great a part as previously. They indicate a sense of tabu by using such expressions as "I found I couldn't go through with it."

Another indication that college students don't think sexuality should be taken lightheartedly is that two-thirds of junior and senior men and seven-eighths of women believe there should be no intercourse before eighteen years of age except in marriage.

Several studies have shown that for a considerable majority of the young women who have had intercourse it was first with men they loved and considered as possible husbands. But a great majority of the men who had had intercourse said they first had it with girls whom they did not expect to marry and did not love. This shows that most girls still very much want intercourse—and sexual intimacy in general—to be part of a significant, deepening relationship. It also indicates either that most boys are having intercourse with a very few promiscuous girls, which was true long ago but I doubt is true today, or that girls, because of their need to feel loved, are still persuading themselves that their lovers are more serious than they actually are.

Recently there has been an increasing number of unmarried couples who live together in colleges where this can be managed without arousing the college authorities and the parents. Sometimes called "The Arrangement," it most often begins in junior or senior year. Studies show that this is usually not a predominantly physical or exploitative affair. It is based on love and compatibility. Often it leads to marriage. The people involved are usually thoughtful, conscientious types. They give the impression to others of being a long-married couple. This arrangement differs from a conventional case of falling in love and getting married mainly in that the couple live together from an earlier stage of the relationship, before they are ready for an open commitment. Many of them, in describing how they came to set up joint housekeeping, speak in an unromantic manner. They drifted into it, they imply. This seems an understatement for a kind of relationship that so often leads to marriage. If this arrangement comes to be accepted and brings about any reduction in the divorce rate and in the number of children of divorce (since the couple generally won't marry and have children until they are quite sure of their relationship), it might become a conventional path to marriage. It is somewhat similar to the "Companionate (trial) Marriage" proposed a couple of generations ago by a Judge Ben Lindsey.

Few college men and fewer women, studies show, approve of promiscuity, in the sense of being intimate with a number of partners in the same period of time or in rapid succession; they believe that sexuality should be reserved for one person with whom there is an ongoing relationship, whether the affair is very serious or only mildly serious. To be sure, there is a small proportion who are actually promiscuous but most of them, especially the girls, are troubled about this and feel that it is not in conformity with their standards in other respects. (Psychiatrists use the adjective compulsive, as in compulsive promiscuity, when a neurotic individual finds himself repeatedly doing something contrary to his conscious wishes and plans.)

It seems significant to me that those particular college men who deny in cynical tones any tender affection for those with whom they become intimate often use disparaging terms for them. This means, from a psychological viewpoint, that they feel scorn not only for their partners but for themselves, because they sense that they are violating their own standards.

The attitudes I've listed here tend to confirm my impression that the inclination (whether slight or compelling) to reserve sexual love for the well beloved is not an outdated convention nor an invention of religious authorities but an aspect of human nature. This is not to deny that people have strong impulses toward casual physical sexuality and that many become involved. I'm only making the point that this is not the basic pattern for man; it is a deviation, however common, of a highly intricate emotional and spiritual system, a deviation that is particularly frequent in adolescence and youth before a fully mature love has been reached. To put it another way, the individual who in early childhood was inspired by idealized images of his two parents and of their mutual devotion (on which he was utterly dependent) won't ever shed completely a feeling that his own sexual and romantic love is intended for a spouse, as an integral part of a lifelong family relationship. On this pattern the survival of the species has always depended, and there is enough power in it to hold most marriages together for life.

Adolescents and youths who have been raised by idealistic parents and who are not ready yet for a commitment will continue, even in a sexually liberal period, to be tugged by contradictory impulses: On one hand the insistent glandular pressure, the gnawing curiosity, the compulsion to learn how to make out; on the other the inhibitions against getting involved too deeply or too fast (including the cautious man's worry that a girl will consider his attention a commitment before he is ready for that), uneasiness about losing self-respect, the desire, strong or faint, to reserve intimacy for the beloved.

When the relationship between two young people moves in the direction of more affection, tenderness, respect, sharing of interests, then the progress of physical intimacy is controlled by those feelings.

I may seem to have overemphasized the college group. I may also have given the impression that I think there is a moral distinction between intercourse and other intimacies and that I've been pleading for celibacy. I've focused on the college group because it's they who have the highest proportion of the sexual inhibitions and worries—and incidentally are the subjects of the most studies.

I certainly could not suggest any one morality in sexuality since it is a highly individual matter that depends primarily on upbringing. However, the studies do show that among the college group the tabu against intercourse is stronger than that against other "normal" intimacies, so intercourse is the critical activity to be analyzed. I have been expressing the belief, though, that sexuality has always been a moral matter for almost all human societies and individuals and always will be. The attempt to reduce it to a simple pleasure like eating can only cause misunderstandings.

One aim of this discussion has been to make clear the nature of the inner conflicts, not because this will end them but because it should make for more satisfactory solutions. The other is to reassure those unready for a commitment, for an affair or perhaps even for lesser intimacies, that a slow, reserved pattern of sexual maturation has been characteristic of many of the world's productive people, most of whom become good lovers, too.

A Reactionary View of Obscenity and Brutality

For decades I was an uncompromising civil libertarian and scorned the hypocrisy usually involved in the enforcement of obscenity laws. But recent trends in movies,

literature, and art toward what I think of as shock-ob-
scenity, and the courts' acceptance of it, have made me
change my position somewhat, particularly in view of
other brutalizing trends.

Civil libertarians have argued their objection to censor-
ship and to obscenity laws on several bases: that there are
no such fixed entities as obscenity or propriety since inter-
pretations keep shifting with time and place; that what is
honest and morally well-intentioned is apt to be penalized
and what is sniggering escapes; that there's no proof that
obscenity ever depraved anyone; that if children need
protection it's up to their parents to provide it. There's
considerable truth in all these claims. But they don't
touch on any of the positive reasons for obscenity laws or
standards.

In the climate of the mid-twentieth century in America,
sophisticated citizens and the higher courts have rapidly
pushed back the boundaries of what is considered obscene. Very little territory is left—"hard-core" pornog-
raphy—and the boundary seems still hard to determine.
In the case of Ralph Ginzburg's publications the Supreme
Court had to rely on the smirking tone of the advertisements in order to decide that lewdness was intended.

The civil libertarians with whom I've argued don't
admit that any form of art or entertainment that they've
seen is obscene or detrimental. But their personal reactions don't erase my doubts, since sophisticated people
take pride in refusing to be shocked. However, if pressed
they'll agree that there are certain acts—excretory or
amatory, for instance—that they might consider offensive
if carried out or crudely depicted in public. This admission—that a citizen's sense of decency can be offended—is
the crux of my viewpoint.

To justify legal or customary standards of decency I don't think it should be necessary to prove that adults have committed sex crimes or that adolescents have lost their virtue as a direct result of reading a story or looking at a picture. No single experience will make that difference. However, various psychological observations have shown clearly that people's standards are always being modified—sometimes down, sometimes up—by the ethical atmosphere in which they find themselves. This applies to sexual behavior and to violence. Experiments have proved that after viewing films of violence, people become at least slightly more cruel in their relations with others.

Man raised himself from barbarism by visualizing higher values and by inhibiting and sublimating his cruder drives. His values shift of course as he gains new insights into the universe and into himself, as his means of existence change and as styles swing. He tries to live up to his values at his better moments, and he tries to buttress them with social and legal codes. These are for the benefit particularly of children because of the sensitivity of their feelings and their trust that adults will give them guidance. Codes are also to restrain those particular adults who have little in the way of standards or self-discipline. I'd say there is no evidence that the need for such codes has been outgrown. We merely are living in a period when the pendulum of style has swung far from an emphasis on propriety at the end of the nineteenth century to an emphasis on tolerance today.

In previous times it was relatively easy for parents with idealistic concepts of sexual love and a disapproval of violence to keep their children from more than accidental exposures to other views (usually those of other children, as most of us remember). Children did not attend theaters unless their parents took them to what was considered suitable. The law and the censor were relatively strict about the books and magazines children saw in the neighborhood stationery store.

The situation is different today. The luridness of what's on newsstands is limited in many places only by the personal ethics of the proprietor. Television delivers progressively cruder dramas in highly realistic form within a few feet of children's noses in their own living rooms. Adolescents from even protective families are allowed to choose their own movies. Yet in a recent federal court decision concerning a film about delinquency that depicted "scenes of brutality, prostitution, homosexuality and sodomy," two of the three judges agreed that, though they were "revolted," the film was not obscene according to the stipulations of the Supreme Court because (1) it was not "designed to appeal to the prurience of the average American" and (2) was not "utterly without redeeming social significance." Another recent film showed a mother practicing a perversion on her child.

In our so-called emancipation from our Puritan past I think we've lost our bearings. Many enlightened parents still have inner convictions but are afraid that they don't have a sure basis for teaching them to their children. Some of their children are quite bewildered, as child psychiatrists and school counselors report. Sophisticated justices are afraid of being considered illiberal. (I'm glad that two of them had the forthrightness to at least say they were revolted.)

I'd suggest that, for public presentations, there be levels of tolerance or tabu. What is allowed to be displayed openly on newsstands and in bookstores for children as well as adults to buy, and what is shown on television during children's viewing hours and in theaters open to all ages, should only be what average citizens would consider not disturbing to children, not debasing to their ideals. This would not mean that immorality, coarseness, or social wrongs could not be indicated, provided it was done in a way that would not crudely shock the average child.

I agree that plays, movies, late television programs, books, magazines should be able to deal seriously or lightly with themes that involve sexuality and immorality—for the purpose of education, catharsis of the emotions, escape, or titillation—without harm to adults over eighteen. I appreciate and approve of all these kinds of works. But I think they should be labeled and reserved for adults. To be sure, some adolescents will see them but only after taking the initiative in circumventing the law or their parents— which will make the experience have a different meaning for them than if society allows the producer to offer them such productions. I don't feel that society needs to prevent adults and enterprising youths from ferreting out erotica from the stacks of the library when that is what they are eager for. The same goes for men's lodges that want to show privately produced movies.

I'd distinguish today a third category of movies, plays, novels, articles, and paintings in which a primary aim is to shock, revolt, or embarrass by explicitly depicting sexual intimacies—especially those of a loveless, perverse, or brutal kind—and other works that horrify with vivid details of nonsexual brutality. Most though not all of these works are obviously feeble in their artistic or social significance.

The motivation, as I see it, of such authors and producers—in addition to making easy money—is the same
particular pleasure that peddlers of lurid gossip enjoy or
that loosely brought up children gain from expounding
crude sex "information" to protectively reared children. I
think such works are unhealthy for society because they
assault the carefully constructed inhibitions and sublima-
tions of sexuality and violence that are normal for all
human beings (except those raised without any morals at
all) and that are essential in the foundations of civilization. These tabus explain why human beings seek privacy
for their own sexual activity and are embarrassed when
they see the intimacies of others, why they are horrified
when they view cruelty. This is not to deny that people
at the same time have a morbid curiosity in these respects.

The abrupt and aggressive breaking down of inhibitions
can be disturbing to a society as a whole and particularly
to its children, even if sincere efforts are made to shield
the children. This seems more risky when a society already
has soaring rates of delinquency and crime, an insatiable
appetite for brutality on television, and what I consider
an unprecedented loss of belief in man's worthiness.

I agree that writers considered great by the test of time
have occasionally and discriminately introduced material
which shocked, in order to confront people with certain
significant social, moral or artistic issues. I agree that a
culture like that of late nineteenth-century America which
had become constricted with prudery and propriety had
to be shocked somewhat in order to be restored to honesty.
That is what happened gradually over a half century:
Judges acknowledged, in effect, in a succession of key
cases, that the social, moral and artistic value of certain

controversial new works was great enough to overbalance the judges' initial reaction of shock.

But I feel that this past process of rectification was quite different from today's situation. Now it is mainly writers, artists and producers with little discernible artistic or social integrity who are leading the assault on standards. And the courts are using as their only criteria for guilt the "appeal to prurience" and the "utter lack of social significance," which are too limited and technical to bar the kinds of material I consider destructive.

Of course I'd be best satisfied if people would decline in such great numbers to support shocking presentations that the producers would give up in discouragement. This would be the ideal way to bring about change without submitting to the arbitrariness of laws and judges. But since I don't believe that an overwhelming revulsion is likely to occur for another ten years, I would now join a majority, if such developed, in favor of new laws which would determine guilt simply on the basis of judges' and juries' sense of shock and revulsion. (I realize that almost no liberals or intellectuals, old or young, would go along with me.) I'd want such laws to specify that they are not intended to discourage the presentation of themes involving immorality, lawlessness, cruelty, or perversion (all of which have regularly been dealt with in great literature and art) but only to curb a shocking manner of presentation.

I do recognize that what is considered shocking or brutalizing will vary with the times. I admit that the laws I suggest might delay the publication of a future *Lady Chatterley's Lover*, which would be a substantial loss in the interval; but its worth would be vindicated in the end.

I agree that my reasoning is the same that all censors and prophets of doom have used. On the other hand, nations and civilizations have actually disintegrated when their belief in themselves and their adherence to standards were lost.

While I'm confessing, I want to add that when writers sprinkle their sentences with obscene words that have no particular connection with the topic but are added for exclamatory effect, it alienates rather than impresses me. There has been a belief since ancient times that trying to strengthen your prose with blasphemies and obscenities (just as with the excessive use of exclamation marks and the word "very") weakens it instead. I think that this still holds true. What embarrasses me is that these writers give the impression that they think they are being emancipated and sophisticated. Actually this has always been a four-year-old style. That's the age when children say to each other "I'll flush you down the toilet" or "You're a pee-pee" and then are convulsed with laughter at how witty and wicked they are.

III
Aggression and Hostility

The most frightening of our problems is how to keep from destroying ourselves with the weapons we've invented. Our difficulty is further complicated: When we're faced with a danger that arouses great anxiety but for which we can find no easy answer, we use the ostrich's solution of ignoring the danger. Though the emotional steps by which we let ourselves become involved in a war are ridiculously easy to analyze and, on this account, should be easy to avoid, few of us seem willing to go through the mild intellectual discipline required; we'd rather enjoy the emotional excitement of being swept up in the war fever. And most of us would rather run the risk of nuclear annihilation than the risk of being thought unpatriotic or eccentric because of antiwar activity.

I joined the peace movement in 1962, during the debate on resumption of nuclear testing. I realized that, as more and more nations tested their new weapons, the fallout would produce increasing amounts of cancer, leukemia, and birth defects in children all around the world. I also stopped denying the danger of nuclear war. I realized that it isn't just a question of: Do you or don't you think the Communists can be trusted to abide by a disarmament agreement? It's that we are all in the same boat—Communists, capitalists, and Hottentots alike—increasing our common insecurity as we seek security through greater armament. I realized that America, armed to the teeth, cocky in spirit, was raising its children with less and less control over their aggressiveness. I thought that if the world is to survive people of all nations must better understand the nature of their own aggressiveness and hostility. I joined the National Committee for a Sane Nuclear Policy, became cochairman in 1964, and spent increasing amounts of time on the road for peace. I campaigned on television and radio for Lyndon Johnson's election in the fall of 1964 because he promised not to escalate the war in Vietnam or to send Americans to fight there, and he even called me on the telephone to thank me. His abrupt escalation of the war three months later quadrupled my anxiety and my activity.

The topics in this part of the book begin with the nature of aggression in animals and trace it through childhood to the adult's self-deceptive hatreds of other groups and other nations. This brings us to the tragic and revealing example of Vietnam, which is only one episode in our country's mounting use of power all over the world. The excuse, the delusion by which we seek to justify our aggression is our anti-Communist paranoia. I see it as fatally distorting our judgment in national and international affairs. It will lead us to self-destruction if we cannot cure ourselves and build a friendly world instead.

Aggression and hostility mean different things to different people. I think of all human beings as being born with the potentiality for reacting with hostility (loosely synonymous with antagonism, hatred, cruelty, murderousness); but how far it is developed in each will depend on the amount of antagonism and cruelty in his family and on how effectively he is taught to control it.

I use aggression to mean a full or exaggerated amount of assertiveness, domineeringness, forcefulness, competitiveness, without the implication of hatred, unless I say hostile aggression.

Are We Better or Worse Than Animals?

Man can be the most affectionate and altruistic of creatures, yet he's potentially more vicious than any other. He is the only one who can be persuaded to hate millions of his own kind whom he has never seen and to kill as many as he can lay his hands on in the name of his tribe or his God.

How can he encompass such opposite traits?

It's helpful, for background, to glance at other species. Konrad Lorenz in his book *On Aggression*[1] and Robert Ardrey in *The Territorial Imperative*[2] have collected recent observations of ethologists on forms of aggression in the animal world. I'll summarize in my words those that seem to have a particular bearing on man. We are apt to think of aggression as mainly propelling one species toward its prey or helping another to fight off its predators. Surprisingly, though, aggression plays a much greater role in the relationships between members of the same species. It is thought to have several positive values.

Aggression against members of the same flock or herd or pack is what establishes the rank order, commonly known as the pecking order. We may think of this as an undesirable kind of behavior because we have a distaste for overbearingness or submissiveness in human behavior.

[1] Harcourt, Brace & World, 1966
[2] Atheneum, 1966

But it must be of vital importance for survival since it is characteristic of so many social animals. It is a stabilizer of relationships because, when established, it minimizes the need for fights or threats. The group or community gets its leadership, its stability, its security from the structure of the rank order.

Aggressive rivalry within a species also fosters a fighting spirit and skill, which can then be used in the defense of the group against another predatory species.

Many species of fish, birds, and mammals defend aggressively the territories in which they live and feed, against neighbors of the same species, though this rarely requires a physical encounter. A bird warns possible intruders with his song, a monkey with his screeching. Some mammals serve notice to trespassing neighbors by depositing feces or urine at regular intervals around the boundaries of their territories. (Certain birds use excreta in an even more directly hostile way by defecating on mammalian intruders with a dive-bombing technique. The hostile meaning of feces shows up in the early development of the human child, too.)

In other species it is not the individual or pair but the larger group that defends its territory against another group of the same species. In different species there are various degrees of intrusiveness or of deference for the territorial rights of others—what Ardrey calls territorial morality.

Presumably the main biological value of territoriality in most of the species in which it exists is to spread the species evenly over the area available for feeding. But there are other species in which, though territoriality puts a little distance between individuals, they remain in clusters, leaving large areas uninhabited. Does this mean that in these species quarreling over territory is biologically valuable merely because it keeps wits sharp? In any case, it is clear that the individual of many species (including man) will fight to keep his territory free of neighbors but still doesn't want to be too far from them.

Man exhibits territoriality when he goes to court on slight provocation over a property dispute, even with a close relative, takes high alarm (along with his neighbors) at rumors that undesirable types may be moving into the locality, argues in dead earnest that his state is the most beautiful one in the nation, tingles with excitement when the chief of his nation asks for a declaration of war, or even when a military band approaches in a parade.

Man is more flexible than other animals in his territoriality as he is in so many other behavior patterns. He may feel threatened by and belligerent toward only an outside group—national, racial, religious, and so on—and trust his own relatives; or he may focus most of his antagonism on family members.

Other animals quarrel, many over territory, some over foods or mates, but their hostility has been carefully limited and patterned, during the course of evolution, into symbolic, ritualized forms of threat and submission, which save blood and lives. They intimidate each other by bristling their fur or feathers, snarling, showing teeth, staring at each other. They admit defeat at various stages of confrontation by looking away, walking away, lying down supine.

Two fallow deer starting a fight first goose step for a way, side by side, then turn simultaneously, lock antlers, and sway their heads harmlessly sideways (similar in spirit to the hand wrestling we call Japanese wrestling) until one is exhausted, at which point the fight is over. But if one turns toward the other too soon, he doesn't gore him in the flank as he could easily do; he hurries to catch up and tries this time to match his turn to his adversary's. When one wolf in a fierce fight is ready to give up, he suddenly turns his head to the side exposing his vulnerable neck; this symbolic submission is enough to completely inhibit further attack by the victor.

One exception to the rule that fights between members of a species are innocuous is the case of rats. Serious fights do not occur between members of a clan even when it is large. But if a stranger rat is introduced into their cage the clan turns savagely hostile and murders him.

Though man has many forms of ritualized and vicarious aggression, he also has psychological mechanisms through which he is released from his legal and moral prohibition against murder and—unlike all other animals—kills multitudes in wars and persecutions, kills relatives and lovers in "crimes of passion."

There are several observations about positive bonds between individuals of certain species that are of particular interest to those of us concerned with humans. In the first place, what draws and holds individuals together in many species is not love. Though minnows swim together in schools they do this in response to a simple instinct; they show no sign of knowing or caring about each other as individuals. In many species of birds, even though a male and female mate, build a nest, and raise young together, there is no evidence that they recognize, need, or miss each other at other times.

Enduring bonds of affection, such as will pull individuals who have been separated back together and make their reunions joyful, occur in relatively few species and only at a late stage of the evolution of that species. What is perhaps most significant of all is that such love exists *only* in species that show considerable hostility to strangers of their own kind. Furthermore, it has been shown that loving bonds and affectionate ceremonies have been developed, during the process of evolution, directly out of hostile patterns. For example, by careful analysis of the emotional meaning of certain behavior patterns of graylag geese, it has been shown that the affectionate greeting pattern of a male for his mate (and he is genuinely devoted to her) has evolved literally out of an aggressive threat pattern toward a neighbor goose: Before cackling happily and affectionately with his spouse he must first always go through the motions of rushing fiercely but briefly toward a neighbor, then make a U-turn to his mate. In graylag geese, love develops only between parents and their goslings and between mates, not between neighbors. However, neighboring families that are ordinarily antagonistic to each other join together to fight off strange flocks that threaten to intrude into their lake territory.

In affectionate species, love of intimates and antagonism toward strangers of the same species enhance each other. When external aggression threatens, positive bonds in the family or group are tightened. And when individuals are with their families they show more hostility toward strangers.

All these patterns are visible in human beings: rank order; territoriality expressed as antagonism toward intruders or as patriotic belligerence; the ritualization of aggression; the close association of love and hate for the same person; the tendency of quarreling individuals or groups to join together when threatened by a more remote or less familiar enemy and to fall out when the danger passes.

Aggression and Control in Childhood

Man is distinctly more aggressive, cruel, and relentless than any of the other apes. The most likely cause is that whereas the others are vegetarians who live partly in trees, man's prehuman ancestors gave up the protection of the forest to hunt other animals in the plains. For this they needed aggressive and hostile qualities, an upright posture, imagination, cunning, hands that could fashion weapons.

Man's aggression and hostility are further intensified and focused, I think, by his suspicious mind and unleashed by his unique capacity to put the blame on others. To show the many-sidedness of these qualities I'll trace their development from infancy. Equally important is to point out how they are balanced and controlled by love.

An infant of three months will greet any friendly human being with such an enthusiastic smile that it makes his whole body squirm. So his core is loving and sociable. There are at least two reasons why, in the evolution of our own species, love became so extraordinarily important. It has to be strong in order to hold the family together during the rearing of the children, each of whom requires nearly a couple of decades to mature. And it is through the complicated sublimation of the child's intense love for his parents that he grows up to become a civilized being who can contribute to the further progress of his society.

By the second half of the first year a child's basic personality is being shaped by his relationship with his mother. All day she interprets the world to him; its usable objects, its dangers, its delights. Through her he acquires his fundamental feeling about humanity and about himself. If she is affectionate, sensitive to his needs, reliable, he starts life with an assumption that all humanity is equally so. His own confident friendliness will in turn evoke whatever friendliness there is in other people as he goes through life. If his mother is cold, unpredictable, hostile, he learns before the age of a year to mistrust all people to a degree. His own mistrust will, in turn, arouse unfriendliness in others.

If his mother acts as if she thinks he is attractive and basically good (even though a nuisance at times) he will accept this image of himself and live up to it. If she herself was brought up in such a way that she expects him— and all children—to be disagreeable or dishonest or cruel, he will respond.

An infant's explosions of rage, when he is hungry or uncomfortable, do not become focused on his mother. Breast fed babies only very occasionally bite the mother's nipple and if she scolds sharply they won't try it again for a long time. My interpretation is that there's an inborn inhibition of hostility in all infant mammals, especially oral hostility, to allow suckling, and that it is only later released by the mother's teaching or the provocation of siblings. Toward the end of the first year, a cranky baby will bite his mother's arm, ever so slowly, eyeing her warily to see what she will make of it. A sensible mother protects herself and starts teaching her child to control his meanness. "Don't bite Mommie. Kiss Mommie." Another mother lets herself get bitten and then reproaches her baby with a half-whimpering, half-playful manner, "You hurt Mommie. Boo-hoo!" The baby watches this bit of masochistic acting with fascination and takes another bite—a minute example of how a cruel component can be built into a relationship.

When an infant bites his mother it is with a positive, possessive feeling as well as a negative one. Actually love and hate are developed side by side in childhood for the same people—the parents, brothers, and sisters—and remain closely interrelated for life. They are not opposites. It has often been said that you don't hate a person unless you've first loved him.

Even in the second year a child who must be frustrated by his mother will not strike at her unless she has been encouraging him to do so. Instead he hits the floor with his head and fists and feet in a tantrum.

A first child of self-controlled parents who has never had a real tussle or an angry fight is apt to be still so inhibited in the expression of aggression at two or even three years of age that he lets other children grab his playthings and only cries. This is very different from the second or third child, who has usually been picked on by his jealous older brother from the beginning. He, by the time he is a year-and-a-quarter, has learned to fight with vigor. In other words a child has to be taught to release the inhibition on his aggression.

Between one and three years a child becomes increasingly aware of his ego and his rights and is often irritatingly aggressive in asserting them. He makes issues when there's no need, just to exercise his power of doing so.

Freud pointed out how symbolic the child's bowel movement becomes in the expression of hostility. Between a year and a year-and-a-half he discovers his movement and becomes as possessive of it as if it were a limb. When, during toilet training, he feels cross at his mother, he may withhold the B.M.; when friendly, he cooperates by yielding it. In the second half of the second year there is a partial shift in attitude away from possessiveness of the movement to some degree of alienation. The child comes to think of feces as a substance offensive to others as well as himself. Angriness may be expressed by soiling. Young children insult each other—angrily or gaily—with their word for B.M. Passing flatus is their first naughty joke. The vulgar words for feces, anus, and flatus are used hostilely by men for the rest of their lives.

How a child and his mother manage his toilet training will play some part in establishing the balance between cleanliness and messiness, stinginess and generosity, obstinacy and compliance, hostility and agreeableness that will characterize his adult personality.

As a child becomes three years old and older his antagonistic feelings towards his parents, if not too intense, are controlled most of the time by the increasing warmth and outgoingness of his positive feelings. He may pretend to shoot his parent dead (and deep down there is a strong anger at times), but he grins broadly when he does it, showing that he distinguishes between real and pretend.

He will also usually be able to express his resentment by words now rather than by crude attack.

Between six and twelve years the child goes back into a more negative, pesky phase as he tries to outgrow his little-boy dependence on parents, and to cast himself as an independent, responsible citizen of the community. His conscience becomes severe and arbitrary. He scolds his father for driving three miles an hour above the speed limit. He suppresses his hostile feelings toward his parents; he can't even pretend to shoot them dead any more—such naughty thoughts make him compulsively step over cracks in the sidewalk. He displaces his hostility away from family members onto groups of outsiders whom his parents or peers teach him he can or should hate, or onto the bad guys in comics, television, and movies. Though he is fascinated with violence, his conscience insists that the good guys must win in the end.

He develops a conscious interest in abstract justice. He even takes pleasure in following rules—not those of his parents any longer but the ones coming from school and the community and the rules of the games that his friends teach him, like mumblety-peg and jacks.

In adolescence and youth, aggression is further harnessed into a variety of socially acceptable activities: athletics, academic and extracurricular competition, occupational strivings.

The style in which aggression is expressed varies, of course, in different social and occupational groups. The man brought up with little education and little coaching in self-restraint shouts when he's talking with other men, uses insults freely, and comes to blows easily. A scientist may have had his drives—positive and negative—thor-

oughly disciplined and sublimated all his life into intellectual channels. His competitiveness may show only in the
slight superciliousness with which he speaks of the research of a rival.

American men generally express their rivalry, aggression, and hostility in the size and horsepower of the cars
they buy and in the way they drive them, in taking
partisan positions in political campaigns, in competing for
job advancement, in identifying with the success of their
organization. They show it in card games, sport participation, sport spectatorship, viewing crime drama on television, reading detective stories, hunting with gun, camera,
or binoculars, contentiousness in the law courts, calling
the police, dish-throwing, fist-shaking, verbal abuse, arguments.

Men vent a lot of their hostility toward each other by
kidding, in which harsh personal comments are allowable
and must be good-naturedly accepted as long as there is a
coating of humor. Kidding is much more common in men
than in women because men have more hostile aggressiveness by inborn temperament and also because they
thoroughly enjoy any of the indirect expressions of hostility permitted by custom—just as two friendly dogs
pretend endlessly to slaughter each other. When women
are resentful they are more apt to speak bluntly than to
bother making jokes.

Psychoanalysis has shown that the strong hostilities
harbored by adults usually follow patterns similar to
those laid down in early childhood and may still be
directed, at the conscious or unconscious level, against
members of the family—who are also loved. For an extreme example: A great majority of all murders are com-

mitted against members of the family; furious husband or
wife kills spouse, resentful son kills father, father in a rage
kills defiant daughter.

Power and Submission

There is an impulse in human beings, as in many species,
to try to dominate others of their kind, an important subdivision of aggression. A certain amount of this is probably essential for survival and to establish leadership
patterns. A baby in the last half of the first year, old
enough to know some of the things he wants but not old
enough to get them for himself, succeeds in making his
mother wait on him for his legitimate needs. This helps
him to gain several kinds of quite necessary confidence:
confidence that he has the right to ask, that he knows
how, that his mother and, by extension, other people will
comply up to a point. The individual who as a baby could
never get his mother to serve him because she was quite
lacking in affection or intuition will probably always be a
sad and ineffectual character.

Mothers of twins can see that one is always dominant
over the other, though the pattern may be reversed as a
result of life developments.

There are at least a couple of routes by which a child
may become oppressively dominant. One is to have a
mother who is timid and gives in to unreasonable demands. (I have known a few babies who were disagreeable bullies by eight months of age; their submissive

mothers loved them and hated them.) The more common way is to have a parent who is bossy; a child in such a situation has to be on guard against being submerged; he also has a strong model to pattern himself after. However, he may have to wait until maturity and independence before he has the opportunity to demonstrate the dominating quality that he has been absorbing invisibly by identification.

Even in adulthood you can see continuing shifts up and down the submission-domination scale resulting from success or failure in work, changes within the family. Some men lose all forcefulness after sixty or seventy.

Men and women have the capacity to submit as well as the capacity to dominate—and they can learn to enjoy both situations, especially if they start in childhood. By logic these roles seem opposite, but psychologically they are closely related. A dominator can sense the feelings of a submitter—that's why he knows how far he can take advantage of him. A bully may become a cringer when up against a powerful adversary; and the toady will usually bully if given a suitable victim. So the tyrant and the submissive person are more closely related to each other than either is to the individual in the middle range who, because of a more secure childhood and a self-disciplined character, resists swinging far in either direction.

The person who has a strong inclination to dominate and is in a position to do so tends to keep increasing his demands until his victim resists, whether it's the college girl who usurps and mistreats the wardrobe of her submissive roommate or the official who bullies his subordinates and the public. To put it the other way, each individual is kept in his place and kept civilized by being surrounded by self-respecting people who won't let him take advantage of them. Of course the individual's self-discipline, built up through childhood, will play a part, too.

The individual working in an organization competes for promotion, salary, and authority. As he nears the top of the ladder his individual identity and ambition become merged with those of the organization, and he strives to increase its size and power. By then, influence and prestige may be as important to him as salary.

The individual, organization, or nation that is succeeding in expanding its power is apt to become increasingly oppressive and ruthless rather than less so. We see this tendency in the operations of racketeers, in the efforts of a giant industrial concern to ruin its rivals, in the tendency of a strong nation to bully its weak neighbors.

No government admits the aggressiveness of its power moves. In occupying a weak country it claims either that that country threatens it or that a third country would otherwise occupy the weak country. It claims it must get control of an undeveloped country's raw materials to be sure that a certain other country won't get this control.

The power drive cannot be eradicated from human nature, I assume. But what we can hope for and should insist on is that men be educated to be conscious of their individual and group power drives, honest in not pretending that these are something else, obligated to discipline them to serve primarily the genuine needs of society.

Self-Deception About Hostility

Much more dangerous than the open antagonism of one individual toward another—for that will only reach the stage of violence infrequently—is the readiness of a majority of human beings to mistrust and hate whole groups of peoples with whom we have little or no acquaintance. Psychiatrists call this displaced hostility. It is derived from the antagonism that was first built up in all of us in early childhood toward family members. As we grew a bit older we sensed that since we were utterly dependent on them we must stay on the right side of them. And increasingly our parents and other teachers made us feel deeply guilty about hating them. So we learned to displace. In early childhood we are apt, in our society, to fear and hate witches, ogres, kidnappers, and other fiends that we hear about and that appear in our bad dreams. By the time we are six or eight we are ready to pick up and carry into adulthood the prejudices of the family and neighborhood against groups of real people. The less we know them in actuality the more easily we can imagine them as evil and fear and despise them.

This characteristic of man has been a main cause, through the ages, of wars, persecution, and quieter forms of prejudice. The capacity for displaced hostility is not the same in all individuals or all societies. Those people raised in the most affectionate and trusting of families can only with difficulty be taught to hate others—known or unknown. There are others so insecure and full of hate that they suspect and dislike almost everyone in the world except their own small circle. Most of us lie between these extremes, having enough insecurity and spare hostility so that we find relief in being able to dislike some one group or other, according to the fashion in our set. If we have been educated to be ashamed of thoughtless prejudice against an entire racial, ethnic, or religious group, we reserve our hostility for those whose views we scorn. We can hate, for instance, those who are racially prejudiced.

War, with the aid of the propaganda organs of government, displaces hostility in enormous quantities; most Americans were easily convinced during World War II that all Japanese were subhuman brutes.

Man has another self-deceptive maneuver, more devious than displacement, which makes him much more dangerous to his own kind than any other creature: his readiness to ascribe what are really his own hostile feelings to the person he feels antagonistic toward.

One man will decide incorrectly, let's say on the basis of a misunderstanding, that a neighbor is antagonistic toward him. The only hostility at this stage is his own. Next he may say something rude to the neighbor or take some mildly offensive action—feeling that it's only in retaliation. Now the second man is apt to do or say something disagreeable in return. Then the first is more convinced than ever that he was right to be suspicious in the first place; now he can dislike and attack the second more vigorously.

In psychiatry this mental maneuver of ascribing one's own hostility to another person is called projection. An adjective loosely applied to it is paranoid; this doesn't mean that the individual literally suffers from paranoia (a mental disease characterized by full-blown delusions of persecution), only that he uses projection in the same way but on a milder scale.

The great comfort to a human being of projecting his hostility is that this process relieves him of guilt—for his antagonism and for any clash that may ensue. The terrible danger is that projection permits individuals, groups, and nations to unleash their hatred and destructiveness.

Even a person with high intelligence and generally excellent judgment can delude himself in such an interplay, as if he had no more insight than a small child who scolds the table when he bumps into it. He blandly puts a righteous interpretation on all his own actions and the worst possible interpretation on his opponents' actions. He operates on the totally illogical assumption that the innocence of his own intentions is obvious to his opponent and he considers his opponent doubly evil for continuing to be hostile despite this.

Another irrational aspect of conflict is provocation. It can be seen with unpleasant clarity during the breakup of many marriages. A husband and wife who once thought each other nearly perfect now see only offensive traits. Each believes that though he himself may have minor faults he has behaved generally well but the other has behaved abominably. One will provoke and infuriate the other with grossly exaggerated accusations, insults, threatened blows or mean, unfair acts. Then, when the other retaliates, the first sees the retaliation as further proof of a malevolent nature. Each seeks out sympathetic friends and details the evidence of his spouse's atrociousness and his own innocence. Their unbiased friends can see how badly both of them are behaving and how ridiculous are their claims of innocence. At unconscious levels of the mind each one does feel guilty, but he resists recognizing this with all his mental strength, for guilt is almost intolerable for the conscientious person. So his basic purpose in provoking his spouse is to evoke such outrageous behavior that he and the whole community can convincingly put all the blame on that spouse.

Other subtle mechanisms are at work here in addition: the pleasures of inflicting and accepting pain; a primitive impulse, when losing contact with a person, to reengage his interest through quarreling; an itch to work a fight up to some kind of climax, an excitement that seeks its own special gratification. The reason that most quarrels don't develop at an explosive rate is because each opponent at each step instinctively tries to pace and arrange his aggressions in such a way that his opponent and not he himself will appear guilty.

The main thing that prevents human beings from destroying each other with their ever-ready hostility and suspiciousness is of course their desire to be loved and their impulse to be kind to others, both derived from the loving they received as children. We all live in some kind of equilibrium between our loving and our hating sides.

But the fatal weakness of man is that though he wants to be loved and to love, and will respond positively even to strangers who approach him cordially, he is ready, if he is at all insecure, to assume the worst about unknown people whose intentions are unclear, such as a stranger at the front door or a person eccentrically dressed.

It is disconcerting to see how arbitrarily man can extend or withhold his kindness. He follows with sympathetic horror the prolonged efforts to rescue one person stuck in a cave or mine but has little feeling about the thousands dying of starvation on the other side of the world. More exactly it is a question of whether or not he allows himself to identify with the person in trouble. There are national as well as individual patterns. Citizens of other Western nations find it hard to believe that in the United States and in England the laws to prevent cruelty to animals are stricter than those to prevent cruelty to children. In the nineteenth century children as young as eight and ten years of age worked in mills and mines in America, twelve hours a day, six days a week, and civic leaders told each other that this was a favor to the children because it kept them out of mischief.

What we do is to reserve for certain individuals or groups our positive feelings and for others our hostility; the rest we manage to ignore. The pattern is different for each of us, but there is only limited logic in anyone's pattern; and it may shift abruptly. A majority of Americans scorned Germans during World War I and during Hitler's regime but felt considerable respect for them before, between, and after these periods.

In our efforts to keep nations from destroying each other we'll have to be concerned not only with the small proportion of citizens and officials who are abnormally hostile but with the great majority who have kindliness but can be so easily persuaded to change it to hate.

Prejudice

The oppression of black people by whites for three hundred years in this country is demonstrably the cause of the poverty, higher disease rates, poor education, lack of middle-class strivings that handicap many of them. But black people are blamed for these handicaps as if they had deliberately cultivated them. When they protest they are called uppity or riotous. Whites who join them are accused of creating the dissatisfaction. Public opinion polls show that a large proportion of white Americans think that black people are now demanding and getting too much, as if they are a specially privileged group. Yet the fact is that they have received in most places so far only token rights to educational, occupational, political, and residential equality; most of them are as much discriminated against and disadvantaged as they ever were.

Almost all psychologists agree there is no evidence of inborn mental inferiority in black people. Mental ability is largely developed and determined by the intellectual stimulation the individual receives throughout childhood. The more education parents have had, the more inclined they are to foster their child's curiosity and reasoning with pictures, stories, creative playthings, trips, explanations, and by answering his questions. These are experiences that cannot be well provided by parents who live deprived, dispirited lives.

Peoples of other nationalities who have migrated in

successive waves to the United States have been treated
badly but have found how to get along here and have
melted gradually into the amalgam. But black people continue to be identified and barred by their color. Those at
the lowest end of the economic scale, feeling no identification with a society that rejects them, have a low respect
for the law, since it is someone else's law and is usually
enforced in a grossly discriminatory way by the police.
This distrust of the law, combined with poverty, poor
education, and disorganized home life, makes for high
crime rates. The remarkable thing is that the majority of
black people remain law-abiding.

Observations of real life situations as well as deliberate
experiments have shown that if any society or community
has been oppressive to one of its groups and then begins
to relent even slightly, the resentment against past injustices, which had been suppressed, will begin to be felt
and to erupt. And paradoxically it may be directed more
at those who have shown sympathy than at those who
have not (in the same way that most people when angry
at the world snap at members of their family rather than
at outsiders). If black people inch ahead in gaining their
rights, more of them will probably become critical and
demanding.

It is an instructive demonstration of man's capacity for
self-delusion that a nation that boasts to other countries
about its dedication to equality and democracy can
blandly deny these rights to a large block of its own
citizens. Or that people who list themselves as followers
of Christ who taught universal love can bar black people
from entrance to their churches. Or that when rioting
breaks out in bitter ghettos, officials and newspaper edi-

tors who have never spoken out against the gross daily denial of constitutional rights to black people declare indignantly that law and order must be restored at any cost.

Groups who have suffered injustice have a strong temptation, when in a better position, to turn around and pick ality groups that were treated badly as immigrants to on other groups that are further down the ladder. Nation-America were in turn harsh toward later arrivals. Members of later immigrant groups have been particularly intolerant of black people. However, this automatic transmission of intolerance can be largely counteracted when parents and teachers help children consciously to master their hostility toward other groups and to transmute it into compassion—as has been shown by a great majority of Jews, despite centuries of persecution.

When the leaders of the more militant black groups came out for Black Power in their conference of 1967, the indignant reaction of many politicians, editors, and citizens had elements of both power rivalry and projection. They took it to be a declaration of war, a threat to seize the country from the whites, though it was no such thing.

The general philosophy of Black Power advocates is to stop asking for integration into the white community, a pursuit that now seems not only hopeless but ignominious; instead black people would use their own political and economic strengths, their skills and courage, to run their own communities, free of exploitation and humiliation by whites. They would acquire political control of the police, schools, health and sanitary facilities, and also ownership of the stores and residences of the neighborhood. Black people—professional, business, clerical, labor

—would as far as possible work in their own neighborhoods.

There would also be courses in schools and universities
on the history of black peoples and of their contributions
to the arts and sciences; the establishment of museums
and cultural centers in black neighborhoods; the wearing
of African clothes and hair styles.

White people need to understand the special importance to black people of control of the police in their own
black neighborhoods. Most middle-class whites have no
idea what it feels like to be subjected to police who are
routinely suspicious, rude, belligerent, and brutal. These
are strong words, but if you will talk with black ghetto
dwellers you'll realize that they are not exaggerations. (A
better way still to learn about unnecessary police hostility
and brutality is to take part in a demonstration for a cause
to which the police have a natural antipathy.) When
Black Panthers began legally to buy arms, to be prepared
to defend themselves against illegal police invasions and
assaults, preferring to die fighting rather than take the
abuse any longer, the police retaliated with intensified
harassment, searches, arrests on fabricated charges. Off-
duty policemen even entered a courthouse to beat Black
Panthers waiting in a corridor.

When the campaign for Black Power was first announced, some white liberals who considered themselves
supporters of civil rights acted hurt and indignant, as if
they thought blacks were rude to spurn their patronage.
Whites have to realize that black people are so resentful
of white abuse, so unimpressed by what any white group
has accomplished for them, that they don't bother with
nice distinctions between different degrees of white sym-

pathy or antagonism. Whites, whatever they think now, have to let blacks decide what policies they consider best designed to bring them justice. Meanwhile whites can redouble their efforts on the political front to get enacted and enforced fair employment and fair housing legislation, to secure better schools, housing, health facilities, job training for black people. Whites have a long way to go in influencing their white neighbors, their churches, their stores and other businesses, their real estate agents to begin showing elementary decency. If whites can in the next few years secure justice for and show brotherliness to blacks, some of the latter may then reconsider their black separatism.

Demographers point out that intermarriage continues to increase and that if this trend continues it will ultimately lead to integration on a biological basis. I imagine that intermarriage, blacks' demands for their rights, and whites' recognition of the justice and necessity of granting these will all be necessary and will reinforce each other in the eventual overcoming of discrimination.

Paranoid Nations

An anthropologist has described the interaction between the people of two neighboring small islands in the Pacific. Each is actually inhabited by people of average agreeableness. But each group believes that the other is composed of predatory, cruel savages. Each reacts to its own suspicions by threatening and alarming its neighbor and sometimes attacking. Yet each is convinced it is entirely innocent of aggression and is acting only in self-defense. The Greeks and Turks on Cyprus who had lived peacefully together for centuries started, when their rivalrous leaders' talk became belligerent, to suspect and kill each other. The Pakistani and the Indians have engaged in a mutual massacre and in a war since partition.

We are indignant when leaders and citizens of other nations lose all reasonableness in a dispute. But when our own country is involved a majority of us will jump to the assumption that all the fault lies with the other country. The United States and the U.S.S.R. have been maligning and provoking each other since the Russian revolution in 1917. In fact, the United States confirmed Marx's prediction about the implacable hostility of capitalist countries toward socialist nations by intervening in Russia on the White Russian side (along with our French and English allies) before the revolution was even over. We refused to recognize the Communist government for fifteen years thereafter. The political leaders of both America and the U.S.S.R. have been insulting each other's country, denouncing each other's faults and ignoring the virtues, threatening to blow each other off the face of the earth ever since. Americans were rightly alarmed when the Russians installed missiles in Cuba. But they forgot that there had already been many recommendations in Congress (and also plans made by the Central Intelligence Agency) for a full-fledged American invasion of Cuba. They also forgot that we had, long before, installed missiles in Turkey, all aimed at the U.S.S.R.

Perhaps a suspicious hostility had some survival value back in the time when tribes fought each other with

spears for hunting territory. But today when so much of
the world has been divided into hostile, suspicious camps,
each possessing a stock of weapons capable of depopulating the globe, man's inclination to hate strangers is no
longer adaptive.

The Perilous Belligerence of Political Leaders

Another factor that fosters war is the way the male fear of
appearing weak gets played out between leader and
people. The kind of man who is able to rise to top
leadership of a nation has to have an acute sense of public
relations and power relationships. In an international
crisis he feels that his courage and impressiveness must be
on a larger-than-life scale if he is to represent the whole
populace. He must try to overawe the enemy leaders,
convince his most skeptical followers that he will guard
them and advance their interests, leave no room for his
political opponents at home to call him soft. So he may
feel compelled to take a belligerent position that his
judgment as a private citizen or as a lesser official would
advise him against. (John Kennedy and Lyndon Johnson
both warned specifically, as senators, against the kinds of
policy in Vietnam that each took, with tragic results, as
President.)

It is also unfortunately true that national leaders have
always felt fully entitled—presumably because they are
acting not for their own benefit but in the interest of
millions—to exempt themselves from the ordinary rules of

decency which apply to relations between individuals. They will lie without hesitation. They will give orders to the armed forces to commit robbery and murder on a titanic scale for which there is not the slightest legal or moral justification.

The leader's political opponents at home can always impress themselves and some of the people by breathing defiance at the enemy and demanding that the leader do more; after all, they have no responsibility and run no risk.

Most citizens will automatically back their leader during a crisis without a moment's thought. They assume that he is right, as children believe their parents are right. The kind of scrappy male citizens who would personally enjoy a fight demand a belligerent policy. Many of the other males, who would fear to become involved in a fight themselves, get a vicarious sense of courage and power by cheering for the leader when he thunders defiance at the enemy. Even a majority of the citizens who doubt the wisdom of their leader's policy will feel a patriotic obligation to present a united front.

The Example of Vietnam

I doubt there will ever be a clearer example of how a nation lets itself in for war—through power striving and the paranoid projection of its own aggressiveness—than in America's involvement in Vietnam.

When in 1954 the Vietnamese people under the leader-

ship of Ho Chi Minh finally defeated France in their eight-
year war for independence, Vietnam was temporarily
divided by the Geneva Accords into two zones, so that the
French and the small minority of mandarin Vietnamese
(rich landlords and officials) who fought on the French
side could have time to settle their affairs in the South. An
election was promised within two years in which the
people of all Vietnam would be reunited under the one
government they preferred. Experts agreed that the
people would vote 80 per cent for Ho Chi Minh, who was
their national hero. But President Eisenhower and Secretary of State Dulles decided that, to prevent the southern
half of Vietnam from voting for Ho Chi Minh, they would
attempt (in violation of their promise to abide by the
Geneva Accords) to replace the French and establish an
American sphere of influence there. Dulles installed Diem
(a mandarin Vietnamese whom he and Cardinal Spellman
had found living in the United States) as dictator of
South Vietnam, in Saigon, and encouraged him to cancel
the promised election.

America's puppet Diem turned out to be an unpopular,
reactionary, cruel dictator. He canceled not only the
national election but the traditional village elections as
well. He gave back to the rich absentee landlords the land
that Ho Chi Minh had previously given to the peasants.
He filled the jails to overflowing with those who did not
agree with him. A major revolt against him was started by
South Vietnamese people in 1960—the Vietcong revolt. It
was so well supported by the rest of the population that it
won three-quarters of South Vietnam within two years.
Our government under three presidents, Eisenhower,
Kennedy, and Johnson—in violation of our commitments

to the United Nations and to the Geneva Accords—took an increasingly active role in trying to put down the revolt. Eisenhower provided arms and money. Kennedy sent twenty thousand "military advisers." In February 1965, when President Johnson realized that the half-hearted Saigon government and army were nearing total collapse, he suddenly escalated the war by bombing North Vietnam and beginning the build-up of combat troops that eventually reached half a million men.

President Johnson kept repeating that the war was caused by "aggression from the North," though the historical fact—confirmed by a careful reading of our government's own White Paper—was that no North Vietnamese army units and few volunteers had come to help the South Vietnamese rebels until after he had initiated the bombing of the North—an example of the aggressor projecting the blame onto the victim. He often stated that we were fighting for the freedom of the South Vietnamese people, though the fact was that we were the main support of one hated dictator after another (Diem had been killed by his own people) and that the only Vietnamese people who wanted us there were the same absentee landlords, officials, and profiteers who had earlier fought on the side of the French against their own people.

It was particularly dismaying to see that all the safeguards that are assumed to protect America against a President's belligerence proved easy for Johnson to circumvent. He broke his promise to obey the Constitution by going ahead without a congressional declaration of war. He said that the Tonkin Gulf Resolution was the equivalent of a declaration; but then the Senate Foreign Relations Committee ferreted out the evidence that his justification for seeking that resolution—unprovoked attack by North Vietnam against our naval forces—was a lie. Our Navy had equipped a Saigon naval force that was attacking a North Vietnam port, with the knowledge and active cooperation of our Navy.

Johnson used harsh, unrelenting pressure against the score of senators and congressmen who initially dared to oppose the war, as several of them told me. He accused citizens working for peace of giving aid and comfort to the enemy. He claimed repeatedly that he would gladly stop the bombing on the slightest sign that the enemy was ready to talk peace. But neutral diplomats revealed that on a half-dozen occasions our opponents did make overtures and Johnson brushed these aside and deliberately escalated the war further at those times.

When our leaders found that the great superiority of weapons and troops on our side was insufficient to bring victory, they resorted to wholesale, ruthless violation of the laws of warfare: We poisoned crops to starve the civilian population, bulldozed whole villages out of existence and put the people in camps, bombed villages with napalm and white phosphorous, leveled most of the cities of North Vietnam and used cruel antipersonnel bombs on civilian areas, turned prisoners over to the Saigon army for torture. All these actions are forbidden by international law.

A majority of the American people took the President's assertions on faith for a couple of years, without checking the facts, as did most members of the Senate and House and the press. Leaders of industry and the professions (including the president of Princeton and the ex-president of Harvard) signed newspaper advertisements agreeing with Johnson's misrepresentation of the cause of the war, as if various segments of The Establishment felt an automatic obligation to close ranks irrespective of the facts.

The President's principal civilian advisers were not Texas cronies or skimpily educated politicians. They were Robert McNamara, a brilliant industrialist, Dean Rusk, who had been president of a great foundation, McGeorge and William Bundy, Eugene and Walt Rostow, who had had distinguished academic careers. The writings and speeches of these officials show them preoccupied with America's power in the world, not with human needs and justice.

Plato recommended that in order to get ideal leaders the state should select the brightest pupils and give them, as an elite group, the finest philosophical education. Johnson's advisers show that there would be no safeguards in such a system. I've always believed that intellectuality that is not balanced by a kindly empathy with people can be dangerously misleading in any field. And fascination with power is perilous unless it is controlled by a humanitarian drive and a touch of humility. I have a particular mistrust, from personal knowledge, of the person who is so brilliant that he feels he doesn't need to listen to other people's views or to question his own.

A crucial question for peace workers remains: Why did Johnson escalate—aside from our government's ten-year-old determination to expand its power in Asia? The most significant reason, it appears to me, was his excessive need to prove virility and to save face. He is reported to have said, when told of the imminent collapse of the Saigon army and government, just before he escalated, "I refuse to be the first President to lose a war." He didn't ask whether it was a just war or even whether it was in the interest of this country. When it later became increasingly apparent that our intervention was failing, he swore that he would never "tuck tail and run." He speaks with reverence of the defenders of the Alamo. He is quoted as saying that nothing gives him a greater thrill than seeing the Stars and Stripes on foreign soil.

I feel that this do-or-die, my-country-right-or-wrong kind of patriotism is not merely out of place in a nuclear armed world, it is criminal egotism on a monstrous scale. The world won't be safe until people in all countries recognize it for what it is and, instead of cheering the leader who talks that way, impeach him.

Add up the totals for Vietnam: a hundred billion dollars spent, forty thousand young Americans dead, a million Vietnamese killed, hundreds of thousands of children orphaned and separated from relatives who as a result will never be emotionally normal, nuclear war hanging over our heads for four years—all so that Lyndon Johnson would not have to admit failure in a power play. Of course his predecessors, his advisers, Congress, and the American people share the blame.

America on the Rampage

Vietnam is not an isolated mistake in American foreign policy. To avoid a succession of repetitions it's vital for Americans to see that behind the United States' involvement there was a power drive. President Eisenhower said in 1953, when we were paying 80 per cent of the cost of the French army in Indochina (the earlier name for Vietnam), a year before the French were finally defeated and we took over: "Now let us assume we lost Indochina. . . . The tin and tungsten that we so greatly value from that area would cease coming. . . . So when the U.S. votes four hundred million to help the French in that war . . . we are voting . . . for our power and ability to get certain things we need from the riches of the Indochinese territory and from Southeast Asia." *U.S. News and World Report* contained an article in 1954 called "Why U.S. Risks War for Indochina: It's the Key to Control of All Asia." The article said, "One of the world's richest areas is open to the winner in Indochina. . . . The U.S. sees it as a place to hold at any cost."

When Johnson and Rusk were pressed as to why it was vital for America to sacrifice so many lives to keep control of South Vietnam, they fell back on their claim that behind North Vietnam is our ultimate enemy, China. William Bundy of our State Department sounded this warning to China: "No single Asian nation should . . . exercise a dominant influence either for the whole area [Far East] or for any major part of it . . . the nations of the Far East should maintain and increase their ties with the West in trade and culture. . . ."

We Americans think of ourselves as good-natured people who have a live-and-let-live attitude toward others, who have enough of the good things without coveting anything belonging to others, who are in fact remarkably generous to other nations when they are in trouble. These things are true of us to a sufficient degree so that they conceal from us the expansive aggressiveness of our military, industrial, and financial institutions.

Actually American foreign policy has always been as aggressive as it had the power to be. Our Mexican War in 1848 was a deliberate effort to steal two-fifths of Mexico. The Spanish-American War was provoked by Americans for a combination of strategic, financial, and journalistic reasons, as well as out of sympathy for Cuban revolutionaries. Our Monroe Doctrine was not for the protection of Latin America, as we were taught in school. It was a notice to European nations that we alone would dominate the Western Hemisphere, which, by and large, we have succeeded in doing, industrially and politically. Occasionally we have felt we had to intervene militarily—in Mexico, Nicaragua, Haiti, and the Dominican Republic. In other countries we supplied the support for revolutions we desired, most brazenly in gaining control of the Panama Canal Zone.

Since World War II America has enormously extended its military, political, financial, and industrial power. It has militarily dominated Western Europe through the NATO alliance. It maintains literally thousands of military bases in thirty foreign countries. By means of foreign aid it has gained varying degrees of political as well as financial influence in a majority of the nations of the world, including even Communist Yugoslavia. It threatens to cut foreign aid, for instance, if a country trades with the Soviet Union or China or Cuba in commodities of which we disapprove. The governments of India and Great Britain could not criticize American policy in Vietnam because they depend desperately on our financial support. Through overseas branches of American corporations and American ownership of foreign industries, our industry has reached a degree of control in many countries—with attendant cultural and political influence—that is distinctly threatening to such countries.

There was a partial justification in the traditional sense for America's extension of alliances, foreign military bases, and financial aid in the post-World War II years, because the Soviet Union under Stalin had occupied or dominated a number of her neighbors. But if you and I are interested in finding not excuses for our country but ways to lessen the causes of war, we have to recognize that the Soviet Union was just as frightened by American military, political, and industrial expansion all over the world as we were by her incorporation or intimidation of surrounding states. And of course the Soviet Union believed, as countries always do when they aggrandize, that their actions were purely defensive.

There has been a gradual lessening of the tensions between the United States and the U.S.S.R. in recent years. But we cannot credit this to greater wisdom. It is mainly due to the growing hostility between the Soviet Union and China and to America's rivalry with China.

When the Chinese Communists won the revolution in 1949 our government assumed they would form a monolithic bloc with the Soviet Union and would challenge our greatly expanded power in the Western Pacific. Beginning then we have taken the position that China is too aggressive to be allowed in the family of nations; that unless we convince her of our superior might and determination in Southeast Asia she will overrun first that area and finally threaten us on our West Coast.

It's good for Americans to imagine how our country

looks to Red China. The United States initiated the campaign to keep China out of the United Nations, forbade our allies and the recipients of our aid to trade with her, armed the Taiwan regime of Chiang Kai-shek and threatened to aid it in a reinvasion of the mainland. We maintain powerful air bases in Okinawa, Taiwan, Japan, the Philippines and Guam, all of them aimed at China. Our reconnaissance planes fly over her. Our Seventh Fleet and our nuclear-armed submarines patrol near her coast. Since 1961 we have introduced increasing numbers of troops into Vietnam, a country on China's border, and built massive military installations there and in Thailand. Our President and State Department have declared repeatedly that we consider China part of our opposition in Vietnam.

Or we can imagine how we would have felt if the Chinese had effectively forbidden most of the other nations of the world to trade with us, had established air bases throughout the Caribbean, had installed a puppet government in the southern half of Mexico, was bombing right up to the Rio Grande, had threatened to help the Russians to recover Alaska and had battleships patrolling off Alaska's coast. We would of course have gone to war with her long ago.

To me it seems embarrassingly clear that the greater aggression and the greater self-deception belongs to my country. It is we who are trying to muscle our way into a continent halfway around the world, not China. It is we who threaten China with a vast, bristling arc of offensive weapons, not the reverse. It is we who have had half a million men in Vietnam, not China.

I believe that the United States should stand up to

aggression of any political-economic color—Communist, socialist, democratic-capitalist—and if the United States has a military alliance with a country whose government is supported by the people, it should go to the aid of that country if asked. I was for the war against Hitler and would be again if another Hitler appeared. At the time I was for America, along with the United Nations, going to the aid of South Korea when it was invaded by North Korea, though I regret that we've ended up supporting a military dictatorship there, as so often elsewhere. But I am opposed to America's committing imperialist aggression and calling it defense against Communism, not just because this is unfair to the country we attack but because this paranoid self-deception can eventually lead to our own self-destruction. For we are fooling only ourselves.

Americans who hope for a more peaceful foreign policy should have a picture of what our government is up to in Latin America, for that is where future wars of the Vietnam type are most likely to break out.

There is serious economic distress in Latin America. A small wealthy class owns the land, resists reform, and shares the ownership of industry with North American firms. There is relatively little middle class. Agricultural workers have become increasingly impoverished due to rapid population growth, low prices on the world market for agricultural products, the high prices workers have to pay for manufactured goods because of the extraordinarily high profits taken by local and United States businessmen—several times as high as profits in the United States. A majority of the nations are military dictatorships. Our Defense Department supplies the arms.

Governments are changed by revolt more often than by ballot. But most of the revolts are not true social revolutions—for the benefit of the oppressed people—they merely substitute one military clique for another. In fact there is no way in most of the countries by which the people could get any change except by guerrilla revolution; this is why Castro is a hero. But our Defense Department provides the military dictatorships with Green Beret units to give instruction in putting down guerrilla uprisings.

Our businessmen and State Department officials have been eager to deal with any right-wing dictatorship. They have been quick to show antagonism to radical regimes that have occasionally come into power through election or revolution and which are naturally interested in land reform, in the nationalization of key industries such as oil or mining, and in curbing exorbitant profits. I was once part of a diplomatic delegation to a South American nation and was struck with how frankly the State Department officials who oriented us focused all their concern on the interests of our industrialists. The needs of the South American people were not mentioned.

For years our State and Defense Departments supplied generous financial and military aid to the oppressive dictatorship of Batista in Cuba. Our industrialists and businessmen prospered there. The people despaired. Protest leaders were killed. Then Castro led a successful revolution through guerrilla tactics. To begin strengthening the economy and reducing poverty he had promised to nationalize the sugar cane and other industries, partly owned by American interests. To pay for them he needed an American loan. After a ticker tape reception in New

York he went to Washington to ask for the loan but was turned down. When he nationalized the industries anyway, which international law permits, our government put an embargo on trade with him—trade from the United States and also trade from all countries that receive our aid—in an effort to wreck the economy and force him out of power. Eventually he got assistance from the only countries left that could afford to give it, the U.S.S.R. and China, and he declared himself a Communist. Americans hostile to him said that this proved us right in shunning him. I and others thought it proved the opposite.

In the Dominican Republic, the American State Department, Defense Department, and business supported the bloodthirsty dictatorship of Trujillo for many years. When in 1965 there was a popular revolt against a successor of Trujillo our government intervened with twenty thousand troops because of a suspicion that Communists might come to play a major role in the revolt. (It turned out that there was a handful of them.) This move outraged the people of all Latin America and will be held against the United States for decades.

When a government was voted into office in Guatemala that promised to give land to the poor peasants the U.S. Fruit Company, the largest landowner, protested to our government. So our Central Intelligence Agency armed and financed a successful revolt by a reactionary military group in 1954.

The Central Intelligence Agency was formed after World War II to unite the spying efforts of the several military and civilian intelligence agencies of our government. It was also given authority and funds to interfere, by plotting and corruption, in the domestic and foreign policies of other countries, the first time our country became officially involved in any such business. The C.I.A. has not plotted against reactionary governments, only against popular regimes that our officials consider too tolerant of Communists or that our industrialists consider threatening to their interests. It helped to overthrow a popular government in Iran. It attempted unsuccessfully to carry out a revolt against a popular leader in Indonesia. In Laos it undermined a moderate leader in favor of a reactionary one. In Cuba it tried to overthrow Castro.

It seems tragic to people who think as I do that when America has become the most powerful country the world has ever known, she has also become, in the eyes of other nations, fearful, suspicious, hostile, arrogant. America, which was born in revolution and which for a hundred and fifty years was a beacon of freedom to people elsewhere, has become the strongest force for reaction in the world today, ready to try to overthrow any government, no matter how popular, that threatens American investments or power.

The increasing desperation of the poor in the underdeveloped parts of the world (more of them than ever before in history) will inevitably lead to social revolutions—by ballot or by violence. There will always be at least a few Communists taking part in such changes, along with democrats, and various parties in-between. The real challenge to the United States is to overcome its paranoia; help poor peoples through bold technical, educational, and health assistance; and thus keep their revolutions friendly toward us. We should help them financially, too, but through the United Nations so that our aid is not used to control or exploit them.

We must not only curb but reverse the drive of our business and financial institutions to buy up the existing industries in foreign countries or to build foreign branches of American firms; our government could buy up these properties and sell them to the foreign governments concerned, on the installment plan if necessary.

Otherwise the United States will end up the most hated and isolated nation in the world.

The Paranoia of Anti-Communism

Why is the world's most affluent and powerful nation, far away from any strong Communist state and with the fewest Communists among its citizens, more afraid of Communism than any other country?

First I suppose is the individualism of Americans. Not that we want to be different from each other—most of us are eager to conform, compared to Europeans, for instance. But we want to be free to follow our own pursuits. We are not nearly as willing as the people of older and more tradition-bound countries to allow the government or other institutions to impose restrictions on us for the common good. We feel we have a right to erode the soil, level the forests, pollute the air, turn rivers into sewers, clutter the highways with hot dog stands and signs, as long as we can make a dollar in these ways.

Perhaps another reason is the firmly held American credo that anyone here may become rich or advance to high position. In a realistic sense most individuals know that they won't, but in another sense they reserve the right. It has always been easy for office seekers and editors in America to arouse an exaggerated fear of Communists and socialists as schemers who want to take wealth away from those who have accumulated it by hard work and give it to the shiftless and envious ones. In other nations, where there is less affluence and where class lines are more rigid, working men have had much less expectation of advancement and so have thought of socialists and Communists more in the light of champions of the poor.

The anti-Communist paronoia has been exploited and intensified by politicians in their quest for office and power. Richard Nixon won his seats first in the House and then in the Senate by implying that his opponents (Helen Gahagan Douglas and Jerry Voorhis) were somehow tainted with Communism, which they were not.

No liberal who is old enough can forget the nightmare of how Senator Joseph McCarthy, starting with his unsupported accusations about hundreds of Communists and homosexuals in the State Department, was eventually able to intimidate Secretary of State Dulles, the United States Senate, President Eisenhower, and almost all the university administrations on which he chose to cast suspicion. Most frightening of all, a considerable majority of the Americans polled believed his accusations and approved his lawless methods. Singlehandedly he robbed millions of Americans of the right and courage to join any organizations except the popular ones—and they haven't yet recovered the right and the courage.

Many American newspapers and magazines were relentless in trying to arouse suspicion and hostility toward Communists in general and the Soviet Union in particular, beginning long before that country threatened any neighbor. They ascribed the worst possible motive to every Soviet action, jeered at the mechanical incompetence of the people, regularly predicted economic collapse or counterrevolution. I think, of course, that editors who believe that a foreign power intends harm have the duty to stir up the maximum alarm. I only point out that most of our press failed to show any judgment in its accusations or any recognition of the part that American belligerence played in alarming Communist nations.

The House Un-American Activities Committee (now renamed the Internal Security Committee) has for decades been traveling from city to city, publishing lists of those people it subpoenas and implying that they are Communists or "fellow travelers," without establishing any proof. This action has often been enough to make those listed lose their jobs. The Committee has exposed little subversion and has brought about no significant legislation. Its real function has been to frighten and silence those with views that it dislikes. The fact that it has been continually supported by a large majority in Congress in spite of functioning in a manner directly contrary to the Constitution is an indication of how far the paranoid sickness has spread through Congress and the general public. There are two similar committees in the Senate.

The Federal Bureau of Investigation has done its part to destroy our intellectual and political freedom. J. Edgar Hoover, whose pronouncements show that he does not understand the meaning of our form of government, has kept up the alarm about Communists and fellow travelers. Careful analysis indicates that those he labels fellow travelers have no connection with Communism. They are assorted liberals and radicals of whose opinions he disapproves. For several years he tapped the telephone of Dr. Martin Luther King, Jr. as a subversive and, after his death, circulated scandalous rumors about him. Recently Hoover has warned America against Students for a Democratic Society, a relatively small and varied group, a majority of whom are as condemnatory of the Communists as they are of the injustices of American society. He has sent agents into the universities, asking students to identify teachers with questionable views, a procedure anathema to the letter and spirit of our Constitution.

I know from personal experience that the F.B.I. will violate the rights of citizens of whom it disapproves. On two different occasions, when peace groups had contracted and paid for buses to bring tens of thousands of people from other cities to Washington for antiwar protests, F.B.I. agents appeared and persuaded drivers to refuse to drive, on the basis that the demonstrators were unpatriotic and that the buses might be attacked by counter demonstrators. This was done at the last minute so that it would be too late to arrange other transportation.

Two F.B.I. agents came to my apartment, on appointment, saying they would like the story of my participation in the peace movement, and I talked to them frankly, having nothing to hide. It turned out later that they were there to get evidence to support my subsequent indictment for conspiracy to aid and abet resistance to the draft. Not getting what they wanted, they gave a report of the interview at the trial that was deliberately falsified to make me appear guilty of the charges.

Our country is already a police state. But the only people who realize this as yet are the groups that happen to have had personal experience in being repressed: black militants, antiwar demonstrators, student dissenters. Congress passes laws to make the exercise of their Constitutional rights a crime. Congressional inquisitors persecute them for their opinions. The F.B.I. spies on them. The police beat them and jail them. Judges set exorbitant bail for the black militants, to keep them incarcerated. Then the victims of police brutality are prosecuted with false accusations of having assaulted the police. I have close friends who have been through all these experiences.

Many Americans think that the guarantee of free speech in the First Amendment is a privilege granted to each of us by a generous country for our own satisfaction. That isn't the idea. The concept of democracy is that the people will be most likely to make the right choice at each step if all opinions are able to be heard and discussed. The authors of the Bill of Rights knew, like everyone who has read history, that the popular course often leads to disaster and that unpopular alternatives should at least be heard. An increasing number of Americans—including myself—believe that imperialism in foreign policy and oppression at home are leading our country into deeper and deeper trouble. If we are right and if government officials are increasingly able to silence dissenters like us, it will only hasten the disaster.

Why Is America So Aggressive?

There are elements in our history and in our character that help to explain, I think, why we have fallen so readily into an aggressive world role. Our country was settled by waves of peoples who had enough toughness and heedlessness to pull up roots and face the known and unknown rigors. We robbed and betrayed and murdered the Indians. We badly treated wave after wave of immigrants. We've continually abused and humiliated black people, occasionally lynched them, murdered them, and bombed their churches. In some frontier regions the individual relied on his own pistols, and vigilantes dispensed justice; our fascination with this half-lawless pattern has persisted right up to the present. We used to chuckle week after week in movie houses at cartoons in which an animal fell from great heights, was burned, was smashed flat, was exploded. Adults and children have watched brutality on television for two decades without ever having enough.

The proportion of war toys in our stores keeps increasing. Our rates of crime and delinquency show no sign of leveling off after twenty-five years of steady rise. Three of our last five Presidents have been shot at. Some school children cheered when John Kennedy's assassination was announced.

So we have always been a rough people, and our aggressiveness has been fostered by its successes. Then in

the twentieth century there developed the revulsion
against the gentility of Victorianism and the determination to no longer be ashamed of our cruder instincts. To
cap it all came the deluge of brutality on television.

Though it is not quite true, we assume we have won all
our wars, and this has convinced many of us that we are
not only unbeatable but that we are always right.

The Cuba missile crisis, with the eventual backing
down of the Soviet Union, confirmed our belief in belligerence. Though I believe that it was an example of the
success of firmness rather than of belligerence on the part
of President Kennedy, and though it is assumed that he
had to give a promise to Khrushchev that the United
States would end its interference in Cuba's affairs, many
of our people interpreted it to mean that if we will only be
aggressive enough we can bully any country into giving
us what we want.

Newspapers print letters to the editor that state, "We
must teach the Communists a lesson in Asia," or "We
should clean up the mess in Cuba," as if no one's wishes
count but ours, as if we have the right and the ability to
impose them by force. Members of Congress declared
from time to time during the Vietnam War that we should
escalate more drastically or drop nuclear weapons, to get
the war over with, showing that they had totally suppressed all human feeling for the death and terror we
were visiting on millions of those people who had never
done us harm. The recommendation of General Curtis
LeMay that we bomb Vietnam into the Stone Age was as
brutal as anything proposed by Hitler's henchmen.

We must face the disturbing realization that as a people

we are only half-civilized in such respects as these. This is particularly dangerous for the country that, because of its supreme power, is able to call the tunes for the world.

Could We Make a Loving World?

We who see the dangers will have to build a political movement that will reject anticommunism and imperialism, and dedicate itself to the needs of people. In the process we must drop the House Internal Security Committee and the Senate's comparable subcommittee, limit the F.B.I. to the detection of ordinary criminals and foreign spies, keep the C.I.A. out of the dirty business of plotting and corrupting and restrict it to espionage. We'll need to recognize China and assist her admission to the United Nations. We'll have to set the example, as the strongest nation, in submitting our disputes to the U.N.— not just those in which we think we can embarrass our opponents, as we have in the past, but those in which we might be rebuked. We must press for a gradual strengthening of the U.N. through charter revision so that it can police the world.

We should help our children better to master their aggressiveness by prohibiting meanness, forbidding them to watch brutality on television, declining to buy them war toys, pointing out to them at each occasion, at home and at school, their natural tendency to project their hostility onto others.

Since human beings so readily become inspired by their

country's past military successes and excited at the prospect of future ones when hostilities threaten again, we should insist that, in the teaching of history, the glorification of war be replaced by the realities of war. Pride in the nation's past statesmen, scientists, writers, engineers, and artists should be taught ahead of pride in generals and admirals. Schools and universities ought to find places —all through the curriculum—to make the students aware of the self-deluding, self-serving, hostility-projecting nature of man—in interpersonal and intergroup as well as in international relations.

Ultimately the only way to prevent more and more nations from developing nuclear arms is for those who have them to begin to disarm. Yet we can be certain that disarmament will be opposed with vehemence by the most powerful institutions and forces in our society. It is the nature of the armed services and the Atomic Energy Commission to be always pessimistic about the adequacy of our weapons and to fight against any restraint. Many sectors of industry, and labor, now have a tremendous stake in the development of ever more and newer weapons. Congressmen and senators are concerned not only with defense itself but with the economic importance of defense contracts for local industries. Every time a new contract is signed the Defense Department permits the congressman of the district to make the proud announcement. The local press features his success. When the Defense Department announces its intention to cancel an order for outmoded arms or to close a useless installation, even in peacetime, labor, industry, press, mayor, regional congressmen, senators set up an outraged clamor.

In any consideration of a possible step in disarmament

(as we saw in the case of the partial test-ban treaty), the suspicious, belligerent segments of Congress, press, and citizenry immediately assume that any proposed decrease in arms will penalize the United States more than its opponents and that the Communists will surely cheat, whatever the precautions. They cannot see that the piling up of nuclear arms has progressively decreased the safety of all countries—on both sides of the iron curtain. They cannot believe that what is good for one side can be good for both.

It is significant that Congress appropriates only a pittance for the work of the Arms Control and Disarmament Agency and that when the Agency's staff members are called to testify, they are treated with open hostility.

There are four approaches to disarmament that can be worked at simultaneously, I think: (1) the patient thrashing out, between experts of the major powers, of actual methods that will minimize various countries' fears of being taken advantage of by each other; (2) simultaneously, the strengthening of the United Nations, as effective arbiter and as military policeman; (3) the education of citizens to elect public officials truly dedicated to the pursuit of peace and to back them when the crucial debates occur; (4) the building of more and more ties between rivalrous countries—cultural, scientific, governmental, and citizen-to-citizen.

America could save its skin and its soul by devoting its energies to the staggering problems of the underdeveloped world. It is difficult for us to realize the appalling fact that there are more hungry and miserable people on the earth today than there have ever been before. They are begging for our food and goods, for our educational, medical, and industrial skills, and for capital with which to develop their own industries. They will have to depend mainly on us for technical help in their efforts to limit their future populations. We have a potential agricultural surplus, excess industrial capacity, unemployed labor to put to work for others, in addition to the eighty billion dollars now being wasted on wars and armament. Other billions have gone into beating the Soviet Union to the moon. The contrast between what we're doing and what we should be doing will be judged a monstrous evil by future generations.

Even in our own country the problems of poverty, racial hatred, poor housing, inadequate educational and health facilities have had to wait for a decrease of our aggression in Vietnam.

In previous centuries when there were plagues or famines or depressions there was little that people could do. Now we have the knowledge and the means to help rebuild the world. We are bogged down because we don't have the imagination, the gumption, the boldness of spirit to get started. If America turned its energy to saving the world, the Communist nations would have to follow suit to compete with us, just as they did in developing the bomb.

Our greatest hope is our children. Children aren't afraid of new ideas. They respond to a cause with idealism. Our schools and churches should prepare them to see the world's needs and to do their part—as workers and as voters. Significant numbers of youths are already showing a fine balance of realism and idealism. They see no reason why they should go along with the present cruelty, stupidity, and greed. They are already at work helping poor and black people to find ways to help themselves. Hundreds are in prison because they wouldn't kill in Vietnam.

As parents and teachers we need to bring up more of our children with generosity of spirit. In other parts of the world they grow up with a strong sense of obligation either to God or country or family. Here we have given them the idea that their success and happiness as individuals is the prime goal. If we could put a greater emphasis on loving service, they would have a better chance, when their turn comes, of making stable marriages, of living more harmoniously with other groups in the community, and of being happy people—as well as of saving the world.

IV
The Psychology of
Political Attitudes

There are discussions of a variety of topics in this part: the less rational aspects of the motivations of conservatives, liberals, and radicals, the drift toward conformity with advancing age, the values in enabling the residents of each neighborhood to have the maximal political and economic control of it, the radicalization of youth today, the increasing reaction and repression, and finally some political planks for a radical party.

So that the reader can glimpse my biases I should explain that I was raised a Republican, in New Haven, Connecticut. My father, a railroad lawyer, told me, in my first election in 1924, that Calvin Coolidge was the greatest President the United States had ever had. So, never having heard any contrary idea at college (Yale) or anywhere else, I pulled the Republican levers down.

When I was halfway through medical school I got married, transferred to Columbia University, and Jane and I lived in New York for the following twenty years. Here I had a few medical school classmates who were Democrats and Socialists, and I was amazed to hear that there were tenable arguments for such allegiances. When the 1929 depression had settled in, wiping out the life savings of many of our parents' generation and throwing lots of our own friends out of work, I, like many in the 1930s, became preoccupied with political and economic theories. I found I was arguing all day as a conservative against my new liberal and radical friends and then turning around in the evenings and using their arguments against my conservative college friends. Why, I'd ask Jane, does everybody seem to want to argue with me? After several years of this, and with the aid of my psychoanalytic training, I realized that it was my own uncertainty that was making me provoke arguments with everyone. I settled down as a New Deal Democrat, which I remained, more or less, until recently.

When I became involved in the peace and disarmament movement in 1962 and faced the fact that we are all at the mercy of the military-industrial complex (and its auxiliaries—Congress, labor, and the press), when I recognized that the war in Vietnam is only one episode in the tireless effort of American industry and government to increase their control over other parts of the earth, I decided that we are not likely to save the world by attempting to reform the old parties, which are financially so indebted to business, but must build a new political movement that will be unambiguously anti-imperialist and responsive to human needs.

Reactionaries, Conservatives, Liberals, and Radicals

These opinions on the psychological aspects of various political positions are not meant to be condescending. They are only intended to show that emotional factors are as potent as any others in determining allegiances, so that we can use this knowledge in the pursuit of our political objectives.

To analyze the psychological roots of conservatism or liberalism or radicalism tells nothing about the appropriateness of any of these positions. The appropriateness depends on the situation prevailing; and it usually remains controversial, anyway, until it can be judged in the perspective of history. Most of the progress in political action is initiated by the liberal and radical spirits. When tyranny or economic depression are severe, liberal or radical leaders step forward and are hailed by a majority. Then conservative leaders appear obstinate and stupid. When times are good, the radical looks like a malcontent to the majority and the liberal takes a more conservative position.

I use the term radical for left-of-center people who are ready to go to the roots of the problems of society—in analysis and cure. (Radicalism does not imply violence, as some think.) By liberals I mean humanitarians who shrink from drastic solutions, often because of divided loyalties or ambivalent personality. So I'm separating liberals and radicals primarily on a psychological basis. There are a hundred subdivisions of each. I'll arbitrarily use the word progressive when I need a term to cover both radical and liberal, though most radicals would consider it too mild a label.

Progressives are regularly frustrated by two major problems: the cleavages and fights within their own left spectrum, and the existence of enough conservatives to block their efforts much of the time. Why do conservatives have to be like that?

Studies from a number of Western countries agree that the greater the amount of a person's property and income, the more likely he is to vote conservative. This tendency is obviously, among other things, a manifestation of territoriality.

A child of one or two years is instinctively selfish about his possessions. As he later develops an outgoing affectionateness, he finds the joys of sharing and giving. The extent of this shift to generosity varies greatly in different individuals depending on the natural generosity of the parents, whether they teach generosity, whether they accomplish toilet training without prolonged conflict. The kind of affluent parents who are emotionally preoccupied with possessions can't help but emphasize property rights in raising their child. Before he is two they are warning him with more than average earnestness not to touch another child's toy "because it's his"; and by the time he's sixteen they put him on guard against adventuresses who will try to marry him for his money.

A conservative feels threatened by the poor and by the politician who speaks for the poor. He assumes, on an emotional basis, that if they get more, he will have less, despite the denial by economists that this is usually so. (When you improve the condition of poor people or nations, everyone benefits.) Whether the country is involved in depression or inflation, war or peace, conservative politicians always see a necessity to cut back on welfare programs.

Most Republicans and southern Democrats in Congress, in order to limit federal deficits during the unprecedented prosperity of the Vietnam War period, fought to reduce benefits for the poor rather than increase income and profit taxes. They sincerely thought that making the poor pay for the war was "cutting out unnecessary expense."

When during the Great Depression the federal government first began supporting large-scale welfare and madework programs, the Republican paper in New York, *The Herald Tribune,* protested that unearned income is always deeply demoralizing, forgetting that most of its affluent readers lived at least in part on such income.

Humans can always rationalize the position that's emotionally comfortable. In the first third of this century the Supreme Court repeatedly divided on the issue of property rights versus human rights, and each side always found plenty of compelling legal precedents for its position.

People will fly in the face of reality in clinging to an emotional position. When Franklin Roosevelt took over from Herbert Hoover at the bottom of the depression in 1933, the average yearly income of physicians in the United States had fallen to nearly five thousand dollars. When Harry Truman yielded to Dwight Eisenhower twenty years later, the average had climbed to over twenty thousand dollars. Yet throughout those Democratic years the American Medical Association spoke and a great majority of physicians voted as if the Democrats were their sworn enemies, out to impoverish them.

The average conservative in his own personal circle—as parent, as friend, and even as immediate employer—can be as genuinely kindly and considerate as anyone. But if the people who need his generosity are remote and invisible—mothers and children living on welfare at a demoralizing level, for instance—the conservative's concern for low taxes keeps him from hearing or believing that such conditions exist. In the early 1930s I met the head of a huge industrial empire who was fighting unionization bitterly and brutally. He was sure that the workers were lazy, grasping rascals who if unionized would ruin him. But I saw him show impressive respect and thoughtfulness toward the chauffeur who drove his car.

Conservatives do not nearly as often as progressives get involved in ideological wrangles. They keep their minds on the action that affects their possessions and power. The high-sounding generalities with which they justify their actions are afterthoughts.

There is social value in the conservative spirit, of course. It helps to preserve the best of the past and to keep change from being thoughtless.

Reactionaries are frightened, hostile people whose thinking is primitive and whose solution for unrest is repression. They are much more aggressive, less self-disciplined than conservatives. Reactionary leaders and their most forthright followers are often members of the lower middle class who feel threatened by the pressure of those lower on the scale for social change and want to

stomp on it. But some upper-middle-class people are also
reactionaries, those who are so hostile in personality or so
used to having their own way that they are quite willing
to be ruthless.

The progressive's readiness to advocate new solutions is
based on a variety of attitudes, beginning with realism
and altruism. A particularly significant factor is resentment of what he considers the unfair use of power by
the authorities—in government, industry, the university;
he identifies with the underdog. This resentment has often
been traced back in psychoanalysis to the individual's
childhood. A small boy's rivalry with his father cannot be
successful, not at least until he reaches adulthood. At the
unconscious level he feels a chronic grumpiness, small or
great, about his father's advantage in size, power, and
privileges. This envy tends to be accentuated in adolescence and youth. A girl feels the same way about her
mother. Through this mechanism a progressive individual
becomes sensitized to injustices in the *status quo,* which a
conservative conveniently ignores. There are of course
other potent factors determining the total amount of protest, which may vary dramatically from decade to decade
—the relative extent of injustice, for instance, and the
spirit of the times.

The conservative, too, felt himself an unsuccessful rival
with his parent in childhood. But when he approaches full
emotional maturity, whether at eighteen or thirty, he is
the one who makes a more complete identification with
his parent ("I can see now that my father was right") and
has less rebelliousness left over.

The liberal position has always been criticized more

severely by radicals than by conservatives. Radicals say that liberals fail to gain their objectives because they don't analyze the political situation with enough skepticism or depth, that they put too much faith in politicians who give lip service to liberal objectives, that liberals always vote in elections for the candidate who is merely the lesser evil rather than work in the primary for a better man or vote for a radical, that they are too easily scared off from working in alliance with radicals for limited objectives when the radicals come under attack.

Liberals often give justification for these criticisms. On the other hand, a majority of sincere liberals are motivated primarily by generosity and fairness toward humanity that, I'm convinced, are among the more dependable attitudes in the long run. What progress has been made in America in strengthening social welfare, limiting capitalist abuse, spreading social justice has been won by the hard work of liberals, despite their cautiousness, though they have sometimes taken their ideas from radicals.

In ordinary times, a considerable proportion of those who join and lead radical movements may have critical, assertive personalities. (So may conservatives and liberals, of course.) These traits are the defects of their virtues, the ones that make it possible for them to analyze issues sharply, come to unpopular views, stand up to attack from right and left—from foes and friends. These are positions that people who are thoroughly agreeable shrink from taking. But nowadays the situation is different. Millions of young people at the college and high school level, without character traits that would predispose them to an extreme position, have been outraged and

radicalized by the war in Vietnam, the brutality of the
police in attacking black and white protesters, the often
hypocritical attitudes of their educational institutions and
of The Establishment generally. I have become acquainted
with thousands of them in demonstrations and in visits to
universities and schools. A great majority of them are
quite obviously unhostile, loving people who are dedicat-
ing themselves to the betterment of the country and often
taking great risks.

A curse of controversial causes and of political movements to the left of center is the tendency of their ad-
herents to break into small factions that often quarrel
with one another more bitterly than they oppose their
major adversary. Older people remember the noisy conflicts in the 1930s between various Communist and Socialist groups in America none of which, as a result, made a
significant contribution to the course of events. In the
1960s the radical youths, the civil rights movement, and
the peace movement that altogether added up to an
unfortunately small fraction of the population were
divided into dozens of organizations. Ideological and policy differences also pitted members of the same organizations against each other.

Why this fratricidal drift? It has a lot to do with the
disposition of hostility. Quite a few of the people who
become militants in an unpopular movement have on the
one hand considerable aggressiveness and on the other a
strong conscience. Their consciences will demand that
they be able to justify whatever degree of criticalness and
antagonism toward the authorities and their fellow citizens they come to. This makes them hairsplitters. And
because they feel disapproved of by the majority and

perhaps by many of their friends, they have a strong impulse to defend themselves by counterattack.

If after long soul-searching an individual decides he can join a group or take a position eleven degrees to the left of center, he may be highly critical of those who are twelve degrees to the left of center. He may say that they are too aggressive, that they are irresponsible because they won't cooperate with moderate groups, that they no longer believe in working through the American democratic system. He is exaggerating the distance between himself and those to the left of him, basically to excuse himself for not having had the daring to go that far and also to protect himself from the more intense criticism that the more radical group will be subjected to.

And he can readily scorn those who are only ten degrees to the left of center by calling them timid, muddled in their thinking, dupes of The Establishment, because he wants to justify to his conscience his having gone further; and he wants the credit for his degree of courage that he doesn't think those with less courage deserve.

The unconscious but true aim of those radicals who come to a theoretical position so farfetched and inappropriate that they win no followers is to be able to scorn and quarrel with the maximum number of people—radical as well as liberal and conservative—while enjoying the comforting self-deception that they are working for humanity.

The rivalries between leaders of various groups enable them to further exaggerate their ideological differences.

This kind of infighting is deeply destructive to any movement. Different groups working for a cause may well find it impossible to amalgamate; but by becoming more sophisticated about the neurotic temptation to quarrel they could learn to cooperate in well-defined areas. At the very least they should refrain from the costly self-indulgence of mutual assault.

Radicals and liberals are unhappy that so many of the youths who are disgusted by the multiple injustices of today and who are devoted in principle to a salvation through brotherly love are essentially apolitical—in theory and in action. I agree that there will be no great improvement until all those wanting a kinder, fairer world find a political channel as well as other ways for securing it. In the past, however, many liberal political movements have lost their way because of the superficiality of their credos; and many idealistic social revolutions have turned sour because their fanatical, rivalrous leaders felt justified in turning to harsh repression because they were so convinced that their particular ideology was the only right one. So perhaps it may prove a safer way to start a new era with a generation of young people who are primarily and deeply committed to love; then if a political movement is eventually developed which can win their allegiance, its philosophy and their dedication to it may be strong enough to prevent it from abandoning brotherly love—as its aim and as its method.

Political Theory versus the Human Element

Man's tendencies to schematize and idealize—and also to be rivalrous—make him eager to find in his own particular theory or his group's theory the perfect solution to any problem; but they blind him to the defects of what he plans or achieves and to the conflicting ideas of others. The history of medicine shows this as clearly as the history of political and economic systems: A succession of doctrines from ancient to modern times have been stretched much too far by hopeful believers, doctrines that have not only had to be greatly revised but that, while they held sway, blocked further progress. I don't want to belittle this enthusiasm and doggedness of man, for it is how he does make progress. I'm only pointing out that the truth is rarely discovered in one revelation, as he hopes. It usually has first to be conceived in vague outline and then worked out step by step through trial and error.

The leader often has as much to do with the success or failure of a social or political program as the program itself. The power-seeking and self-deluding aspects of human nature crop out under any political system.

Though I believe that capitalist imperialism has been immediately responsible for America's indefensible aggression in such places as Latin America and in Vietnam, I think it is short-sighted to speak as though the elimination of capitalism here would end such offenses. We have seen in the twentieth century imperialist aggression carried out by Socialist, Fascist, and Communist as well as democratic capitalist governments. I agree that we must keep searching for political forms that will control the imperialist impulse. But I also think that we have to admit that it is ultimately an aspect of the power drive latent in every individual and in every group of men. So it must also be attacked in the education of the individual and by progressive steps toward world government.

Communist countries that have achieved rapid indus-
trialization and the elimination of poverty have a right to
be proud. But they have intimidated and occupied their
neighbors. They have had serious troubles with internal
power rivalries, with making bureaucracy responsive to
human needs, with bullying farmers out of their possessive love of their land, with trying to control the creativity
of artists and writers and the thinking of scientists and
citizens generally.

America has made enormous material progress, partly
due to its relatively unfettered capitalism and its people's
enthusiasm, energy, ingenuity, and cooperativeness. But
the main reason it has outstripped other capitalist countries is not, as so many assume, because its system is
somehow superior but because of its natural resources and
large size. Americans who believe that capitalism has
made this country the promised land forget its failures,
which are particularly tragic because they are unnecessary: poverty, racial injustice, poor housing, poor education, and poor medical care for many. Those who consider
America a beacon of free enterprise forget that many
industries—agriculture, manufacture, railroads, aviation,
shipping, oil, mining—demand and receive heavy sub-
sidies from government.

The social welfare states of Western Europe have been
a lot more decent than the United States in giving security
and dignity to those who can't fend for themselves, without relinquishing most of the freedoms that are so important to Westerners. There is every indication that in
America, too, as the population grows, as the structure of
the economy becomes more complex and centralized, as
transportation and sanitation increase in difficulty, as in-

dustries ignore the common good, government will have to play an ever greater role as provider of health, education, and welfare; as regulator of industry; as social planner; as owner of certain industries. (Opponents of socialism often forget that, even in the United States, government runs defense, schools and many universities, postal service, highways, public health, sanitation, police, fire prevention, many bus and power companies, space exploration, atomic energy.)

Democracy appears to me potentially a higher form of political organization than any kind of dictatorship. But if it turns out that in America, which could afford a decent living for everyone, the comfortable majority is willing to condone the misery and abuse of a minority for an indefinite period, then exploitation by the majority becomes as repugnant as exploitation by an oligarchy, and democracy loses half its supposed superiority.

Liberals and radicals since the Industrial Revolution have idealized the warmly human attitudes of working-class people and contrasted these with the hardhearted character ascribed to the capitalist. Now, under different conditions and for understandable reasons, many American labor groups are militantly antiblack, antiradical student, and pro-war.

It seems wiser to me to start by admitting that there are constructive and destructive attitudes in all individuals and groups—which are evoked by circumstances—and that all systems devised so far are capable of corruption. Then as citizens we can proceed step by step to analyze the institutional and human problems that beset us—but always remaining on guard against the self-deceptions of paranoid thinking.

The recurring question of how far a leader who claims to have ideals can go in compromise has no comfortable answer, but I think the main psychological factors are clear: Almost every leader has to compromise many times. The crucial question is whether the compromise will ultimately advance his cause or if, while saving his position temporarily, it will hurt the cause in the long run. He hurts his cause if his compromises are so indefensible that they disillusion his more militant followers. But to refuse to compromise when it is necessary to the cause is merely egotism or obstinacy. The only person who can afford not to compromise is the one whose defeat—and perhaps even whose death—will advance the cause over the decades or centuries.

The Drift to Conformity

Why do so many of those who are idealistic and open-minded in their school and college years turn conformist by the time they are settled down? One obvious answer is that family responsibilities impose caution. Another is the weakening of youth's rebelliousness as he achieves his own identity. Perhaps just as fundamental is the fact that the human being, like other species, is designed to be eagerly explorative in body and spirit in childhood, so that he will take full advantage of all opportunities to learn, and then he calms down further at every subsequent stage.

You can also say that a human being is strongly motivated to pattern himself after an ideal figure but that the ideal shifts at different stages of development. In the early years the child strives to be like that glorious, powerful being, his parent. Between six and twelve his immediate pattern for imitation is his contemporaries; his remote ideal is the superhuman hero of the comics or fiction or history. In adolescence, the need to become fully independent of parents encourages a youth to idealize heroes who have defied authority or the contemporary idols of his particular social set.

As the individual approaches full emotional maturity and settles into a job, he looks up to an impressive person in his own field and this often makes for conformity. A revealing example is the resident physician in a children's hospital who strives in the last years of his training to become as much like the head of the department as possible. He is made uneasy by any teaching that seems to differ from his chief's, as if he would be disloyal to even consider it. I, like other teachers of the psychological aspects of pediatrics, have often been foiled by this because the head of the pediatric department in a teaching hospital is typically very much a scientist who, in a majority of cases, is skeptical or uncomfortable about emotions. So the young man who as medical student was genuinely interested in child psychology may become suspicious of it in his second or third year of residency. Later, as the years of practice pass, he often becomes increasingly interested again.

As an occasional organizer for controversial causes I've noticed how much more frightened of involvement the

professionals and the executives are than the more average citizens and the women of all economic levels. The
young man or woman with high ambition invests enormous amounts of work and concern in getting his training
and then in advancing his career. Once he has won his
occupational identity, his basic concern will be to gain the
good opinion of his clients, peers, and superiors by
demonstrating skill and judgment. He thus makes himself—unless he is an unusually independent person—a
slave to the estimation of the community. Many forces
playing on his anxieties push him to dress like, live like,
express the same opinions, and even select the same
friends as those he wants to emulate and please. As he
ascends the ladder he becomes increasingly expert and
recognized, but often in a narrower field. He winces at the
thought of entering a controversy outside his area of
competency, knowing he may lose the hard-won respect
of half his peers.

Another restricting influence in America is the professional or trade association. It is set up by a local or
national group to guard their interests. It hires an execu-
tive. He assumes that to do right by his employers he
should take the most narrow and selfish view of the
group's interests, no matter how much this ignores or
conflicts with the welfare of the rest of society. I think of
the kind of real estate board that always takes a stand
against increased taxes for schools, no matter how de-
crepit they are, the manufacturer's association that is
invariably antilabor and antigovernment, the medical
association that fights any proposed change in the distribution of medical care, without discrimination or
conscience. Some of the members of the business or professional group who as individuals would be inclined to

judge independently the merits of such issues will be intimidated by the appearance of unanimity created by their hireling.

To remedy the conservatism and coerciveness of the professional and trade associations will be a tough job. It's difficult to imagine a liberal group taking over the Chambers of Commerce or the medical societies at the local and national levels—at least until enough socially minded young people have aged sufficiently to constitute a near-majority. But a new spirit of tolerance for minority views and of awareness of community responsibility might be generated if, during this time of questioning and change, the small liberal minorities could spur themselves to attend and speak at association meetings and to contest elections. No such effort is ever without some result.

The same sorts of efforts must be made by the liberals in all labor unions—particularly in those of the teachers, welfare workers, police, health workers, civil ·service workers generally—to make these organizations much more conscious of the needs of the people they serve and of the obligation to help meet them.

To Make the Citizen Important Again

An aspect of many human beings that must be faced politically is that they cannot easily expand their horizons much beyond what they see in their daily orbits. In newspapers and radio news they find interesting mainly the listing of community marriages, engagements, accidents, deaths, crimes, sports. (Suburban newspapers are the only ones growing and proliferating.) It is a distinctly smaller proportion of citizens who can feel a concern for the whole nation and for fellow citizens of different social and ethnic backgrounds. The number who can feel a sense of brotherhood with people all over the world and who follow world news with an awareness that it is the most crucial news of all is minute indeed. To put it another way, the range of man's commercial dealings and destructive capacity has far outdistanced his capacity for empathy.

The best answer, I assume, is to try to keep stretching people's imaginations and concern, mainly through the media of communication. Suburban papers could reach out further for their news and try to keep the distant news lively and personal. Television has the greatest opportunity—and the furthest to go—to widen horizons in the arts, technology, science, societal differences, the political issues of the nation and the world.

A weakness of our democracy that is increasing as metropolises continue to expand and coalesce is the sense of the individual citizen that he is too small and powerless to count. The trend also encourages some officials and civil servants to be impersonal, unhelpful, or irresponsible. It's high time we were exploring ways to break up the metropolis into semiautonomous neighborhoods, in order to return to the citizen the sense not only that the community knows and cares about him but that he has an obligation to be cooperative with his neighbors and to help guide the government. The neighborhood should be able to have at least partial control of schools, recreational facilities, police, zoning, real estate rehabilitation, health, and sanitation facilities. Such a development would coincide with the growing demand among Black Power advocates for political control of the neighborhoods in which they live.

This ideal of man's control of his neighborhood should be broadened to make possible his control of his life generally. Most businessmen and professionals as well as factory and office workers now have a sense of running—continually, joylessly, sometimes anxiously—in a squirrel cage over which they have no influence. In regard to his job a man needs not only a say about working conditions but a sense of participation in the creation of the product or service and in the decisions about how best to meet the world's need for it. In his housing, gardening, clothing, hobbies, and activity in the arts he should have opportunities to express his own creativity. In his reading and television viewing he ought to have true diversity to choose from.

Challenge to Industry

Since the beginnings of industry and commerce in the dim past man has been operating in an economy in which scarcity sets prices, wages, and production quotas. Profit has been the main criterion of success. In the developed countries, at least, we are moving toward an economy of abundance and automation in which more and more goods can be created with fewer and fewer man-hours of labor. If industry's main concern in the future continues to be profits, and if it can produce in the future all the goods men are accustomed to, with a small fraction of the present labor force, then most of the rest of the workers would be unemployed and unable to buy the products. So other social values will now have to play a significant part in the motivation of industry. Also, if the underdeveloped regions are to be kept from succumbing to starvation and chaos, a broader vision will be essential in the distribution of the output of industry and agriculture.

The ruthlessness of nineteenth-century industry has been partially curbed in America by antitrust laws, profit taxes, labor relations laws, the Securities and Exchange Commission, and other federal regulatory commissions. In the same period, however, American industry has become more of a threat to the well-being of the country and the world in certain respects. Its ownership has been concentrated into still fewer hands, despite antimonopoly laws. Its involvement in armament production has tied it tightly to the Pentagon as well as to those elements of Congress, labor, and the press concerned with defense industry—an enormously powerful combination the interests of which unfortunately are advanced by international suspicion, depressed by amity.

Industry has the skills and creativity to satisfy many more of men's needs and the needs of many more men. It has shown that it can, when it wants to, wield enormous influence in the community for fair employment, fair housing, better recreation, better schools, the rehabilitation of cities. Its management has been considerably professionalized in this century. Can it go further and be moved by such visions as the pursuit of peace, full employment, material plenty for all Americans and then for all the world?

It's heartening that increasing numbers of young men and women today are looking primarily for work in which they can feel they are serving people, rather than for salary and security, which, questionnaires showed, were the prime considerations in the 1950s. Recruiters from industry are now not making their quotas among university graduates.

Perhaps these forces working together may spur industry to take on a broadly social motivation in which profit is only one component. The alternative—sooner or later—will have to be increasing government control and ownership.

Factors in Change

I've come to realize, in watching the opposition to the war in Vietnam, the changes in the Freedom Movement, and the rise of student protest, in what roundabout ways movements get their ideas, their leadership, and their results. Here are three small examples. The radicals opposed to the war—predominantly youths—moved from demonstration to confrontation and from symbolic civil disobedience to open draft resistance and refusal to obey orders of the military. The cautious groups in the Peace Movement declined to participate with them because, they said, at each particular stage, "This time you are going too far!" But the cautious ones did become, step by step, more active and slightly more militant. Other people who earlier would not join in any peace activity came in behind the cautious ones. It was as if the radical segments by moving repeatedly to the left kept making room for moderates to join. And though the moderates would deny they were following the radicals, I'd say that they were.

When Stokely Carmichael was the leader of SNCC (Student Nonviolent Coordinating Committee) a friend of mine asked several questions of a black woman friend. What did she think of Whitney Young of the Urban League? "He lives in New Rochelle!" she answered scornfully, meaning that a black leader should live with his people. What about Dr. Martin Luther King, Jr.? "He's wonderful!" she said. Stokely Carmichael? "He's much too wild!" she answered. A few months later I was at the tenth anniversary meeting of the Southern Christian Leadership Conference in Dr. King's church and saw its corridors hung with posters which said, "Black is beautiful and it's so beautiful to be black." This assertion was one aspect of the call for Black Power, which came originally from SNCC and Stokely Carmichael. In this example SCLC was following the leadership of SNCC, though the woman who thought Stokely Carmichael was too wild didn't realize it.

The protest and reform movements in various universities have been initiated by small and often radical groups. But by dramatizing significant injustices—and sometimes by having their heads beaten—they compelled everyone to think about the issues. In certain places

158	*The Psychology of Political Attitudes*

(Columbia and Harvard are the best examples) they succeeded brilliantly in winning a large proportion of the student body and faculty to their position and thus induced the institution to make significant reforms. Yet in most of these cases the student body as a whole would not acknowledge the small radical group as their official leaders, and obviously the faculty wouldn't either.

I don't mean that leadership for change comes only from radicals. Until Johnson escalated the war in Vietnam, much of the opposition to it was coming from politically moderate peace organizations and university groups, and they continued to give leadership to their own followers. All the segments of the antiwar spectrum, each plugging away at its own program, contributed eventually to the increasing opposition in Congress, to the candidacies of Eugene McCarthy and Robert Kennedy, the withdrawal of Johnson, the swing in the tide of public opinion, the switchover of Richard Nixon in the 1968 campaign from advocacy of further escalation to advocacy of ending the war.

In the Freedom Movement the conservative civil rights organizations provided what leadership there was up until the mid-1950s. Then the Supreme Court decision on desegregation of schools aroused hope and stimulated moderately militant activity. The dashing of those hopes has now passed the leadership to angry men who speak the language of the ghetto and who are ready to express the rising fury of the race and take the consequences.

How do you get people to change their political position to the left? Not by arguing with them. Even if they are inwardly debating a change, the fact that they are not yet ready to make it will compel them to counter your arguments with arguments of their own. You can't sway them in a meeting by hostile attacks on a political leader whom they still respect to some degree. Americans shrink back from a speaker who counsels hostility unless they already share his feelings themselves. On the other hand the opportunity for a person, at large or small meetings, to hear others debate the issues, to raise his own questions and opinions without being pressured, can be a valuable preliminary to his conversion.

People most often change their politics when they feel threatened economically or otherwise by the policies of the party in power.

An individual may change to the position of someone he has come to like or admire personally, without necessarily knowing that this is the reason.

Radicalization by Events and Confrontation

By far the most extensive and rapid radicalization in American history has been brought about in young people by events in the 1960s, primarily by the government's policies in regard to the war in Vietnam. However, the early phase of radicalization resulted from the participation by a relatively small number of idealistic black and white youths in the Freedom Movement in the South where their face-to-face encounters with the viciousness of racist officials and citizens and their identification with the black victims opened their eyes to the need for drastic changes in American attitudes and institutions if this is to become a fair country. When Johnson escalated a cruel and unjust war the young were among the first to see its immorality, partly because they are always sensitive to hypocrisy, partly because they are the age group designated to do the killing and dying. They identified with the Vietcong and North Vietnamese fighting for independence. The radicalization of further hundreds of thousands occurred when they saw at the march on the Pentagon, or heard from classmates, about the brutal assault of the United States marshals on hundreds of unoffending boys and girls who were sitting on the grass singing Freedom Movement songs—their own government attacking its critics with clubs. It was easy for them then to see the parallel between foreign and internal oppression and also the powerful alliance of government, Pentagon, and imperialist industry. (Spokesmen for The Establishment refuse to understand what happens on such occasions. They try to persuade themselves that a hundred thousand demonstrators are thugs or dupes of an alien conspiracy. James Reston persists in saying that the march on the Pentagon spelled the downfall of the Peace Movement, because there were a few obscene signs and epithets.) At the Democratic convention the violent police assaults on courageous young people who had every right to demonstrate there radicalized millions of others who watched on television.

The beating of students who occupied university buildings in protest against injustices has intensified the processes of alienation and radicalization because it has revealed the academic authorities, in calling on the police for violence, as morally no better than the police in this respect and as snugly in the same Establishment bed with government, Pentagon, and industry.

The frankly admitted aims of the leaders and participants in such demonstrations are to call public attention to an injustice and show that many are fighting it, to make people who are potential supporters think about the issue and to recruit as many of them as possible, to inspire the existing supporters to be more militant, to publicly shame the institution, whether government or university, and to pressure it eventually into changing policies or changing leadership.

The element of confrontation or defiance—symbolically obstructing the Pentagon, ignoring Mayor Daley's unconstitutional ban, occupying a university building—is designed by the leaders, and willingly carried out by the supporters, for several purposes: to highlight the issue, to make it impossible for the institution to ignore the demands any longer, and to give it the opportunity, if it will not be reasonable, to respond under circumstances that will reveal to the outside world the institution's arbitrary and unjust attitude.

Law and Order

The officials, editors, and citizens who demand law and order as the answer to confrontations and riots are able to do so because they are from groups that are basically satisfied with the *status quo* and alarmed at any prospect of change. With their human capacity for one-sided thinking they can ignore the abusive discrimination against black people that has been flagrantly illegal for a century. They never answer the accusation of antiwar protesters that the war in Vietnam is totally illegal and immoral. They never acknowledge the fact that the students who confront university administrations are not demanding special privileges for themselves. They are protesting such matters as university collusion with militarism, injustice to the university's poor black neighbors, injustice to socially concerned faculty members. And they only take to obstruction after the administration ignores their orderly requests for change or stalls indefinitely in its response.

If the advocates of absolute law and order had had their say in other times women would not have gained the vote, labor unions would not have broken the stranglehold maintained by industry through the court injunction process, there would have been no American Revolution and France and England would still be ruled by absolute monarchs.

All people prefer the security of law and order. But if unjust laws are retained or if just laws are flouted, brave men will eventually arouse sufficient popular support by what pressures are necessary to establish right. This is how much of our social and political progress has been achieved. The signers of the Declaration of Independence said that people have a right to revolt if legal efforts fail. Lincoln reiterated this.

I and others who have been prosecuted for our methods in protesting against injustice have been accused by many people of considering ourselves above the law or of picking and choosing among the laws we'll obey. I've never known anyone who claimed the right to pick and choose

—that could only be the unspoken attitude of an ordinary criminal who had grown up with no sense of responsibility. Those who commit civil disobedience are deadly serious people who deliberately disobey a law that they consider monstrously wrong and are willing to pay the consequence in order to focus public opinion and thwart unjust authority. But that position was not my own when I offered moral and financial support to young men who in conscience refuse to fight in Vietnam. I believed from reading the historians and the reporters that the war in Vietnam was totally illegal. I also believed that the Nuremberg principle—that our government and its allies established and used to put German and Japanese war criminals to death and that declares that if your government gives you orders constituting crimes against humanity or against the peace you are obligated to refuse to obey them—applies to Americans, too. To claim otherwise would be to make a mockery of all law. I believe that the laws and regulations of the Selective Service System are nullified in regard to an illegal war by this principle of international law and that this position will eventually be recognized by our courts. Therefore I believe that I was not disobeying the law but supporting it.

Laymen are apt to assume that the law as a whole is a carefully integrated system that can immediately pronounce whether any human act is legal or illegal. No such thing. There are tens of thousands of laws in a country like ours, most of which are not being enforced—enforcement being left to the discretion or prejudice of the prosecutor and policeman. Most of them conflict with other laws so that it is often necessary to go through several courts to find which law pertains or if a person accused of transgression is guilty. Even the Supreme Court finds the law difficult to determine as is shown by the frequency of split decisions and by its occasional reversal of itself years or generations later, as in the issue of separate schools for black children.

This is not to deny the practical necessity for laws and for enforcement, only to remind those who seriously doubt the applicability of a certain law to themselves that they have the right (if they have the means) to run the judicial gauntlet and need not feel shamed by an accuser until the final verdict is in.

Conservatives, reactionaries, and even some who consider themselves liberals are now in full cry like excited hounds in their frenzied attacks on student militants. They call the militants ruthless anarchists bent on the destruction of their universities and their country. A particularly despicable example, I thought, was the provocative captions on the news photographs of armed black Cornell students that implied that they had invaded a building at gunpoint when it was known that the weapons had been brought them by friends late in their sit-in, after there were credible rumors of an armed attack by conservative white students. Some critics who should know better try to shame the militants by likening them to Hitler's street thugs, the most farfetched accusation of all, since Fascists were racist, antidemocratic, and chauvinistic.

Why do officials and press and citizens try so hard to blacken the image of the young radicals? Many older people jump to the frightened assumption that the just society that the students demand would deprive them of

their privileges or even of their security. They are angry
that young people will not stay in their assigned role as
docile apprentices, an aspect of the hostile rivalry between the generations that is always latent. They recognize in the backs of their minds—without admitting it
even to themselves—that the radicals are idealists; but
they can hate and attack them more freely if they can
pretend that they are fiends.

When Establishment spokesmen and congressional
committees single out Students for a Democratic Society
for particular vilification or persecution they are trying,
whether they are conscious of it or not, to turn the more
moderate student dissidents against all radical leaders, an
attempt to defeat by dividing.

How Far Dissent?

Commencement speakers, editorial writers, and university
administrators are now almost unanimous in expressing
respect—even admiration—for student dissent as long as
it is entirely decorous and verbal. But they condemn any
pressure, any interference with university functioning, as
an intolerable violation of the rights of other students and
faculty.

This double statement adds up to nonsense, with which
the speaker is fooling himself as well as the public. It is
like the mother in the nursery rhyme who says to her
child who has asked to go for a swim, "Yes, my darling
daughter. Hang your clothes on a hickory limb but don't

go near the water." For in a great majority of recent instances of militant action, the students had repeatedly asked in a polite way for discussion of their proposals—to right what they considered injustices—and had been brushed off or stalled indefinitely. It was only when they applied pressure, as by occupying a building, that they won the attention and support of large numbers of other students and faculty members and convinced the administration that it would have to consider their demands seriously.

To put it another way, in the university as in other institutions and in international relations, those who hold control rarely yield any of it, or any significant concessions, in response to polite requests but only when they feel they have to because the alternatives look worse. In fact those in power—and the press also—hardly bother to conceal their contempt for those who ask for something without having any power for leverage. This contempt has been all too evident to workers in the Peace Movement.

Black people learned this bitter lesson in a hundred years of listening to white admonitions and hollow promises. So did working men when they were without unions or the right to strike. So have small nations that are at the mercy of more powerful neighbors.

All this is not a reason for becoming cynical but it is a reason for speaking honestly. If editors and public figures and university administrators really believe that students have a right to a voice in policy—not just an opportunity to sound off harmlessly—they must advocate granting them significant power (it doesn't have to be a majority of

the votes) or stop complaining when students look for a
way to press the issue.

In trying to bring pressure to bear on any administration—university or otherwise—there are two primary
considerations that sometimes are forgotten in the heat of
conflict. The ultimate aim is not to express indignation or
to shame the institution, though these may be incidental
steps along the way, but to right injustice. And the essence of the means, whatever the specific methods, is to
win so many supporters that the administration feels
obligated—tactically and ethically—to grant reasonable
concessions.

Winning supporters usually has to be done by dramatic
or ingenious methods because most people, though basically committed to justice, will try to ignore injustice as
long as possible, to avoid the multiple pains of involvement.

It's wise, I think, to start a campaign with democratic
organizing. A meeting can be called of all those potentially interested, to sound out the extent and depth
of dissatisfactions, discuss alternate approaches, elect
officers and appoint committees, decide on next steps. If a
committee can go to the administration of a university, a
municipality, or an industry and speak for several hundred
people, it is much more likely to get a serious hearing than
if a half dozen protesters can speak only for themselves.

When it comes to action I think that polite requests for
consideration of grievances and reasonable discussions
with the authorities should come first and be continued as
long as there is evidence of good faith. It may secure the
desired result. If responsible requests are rejected on what

seem insufficient grounds or if the administration is obviously stalling, then more militant steps can be considered. Taking the most courteous course to begin with will be comforting to the consciences of those involved, and it will make much more likely the recruitment of supporters —at the start and also later if the going gets rough.

Next can come protest activities of increasing militancy, such as leafleting, picketing, a strike of some kind, symbolic occupation of a building without actual obstruction, obstruction of a disapproved recruiting organization, brief obstruction of an administration building, prolonged obstruction. The more aggressive actions obviously carry greater risk of penalties unless they gain such strong support that the administration feels blocked. So the rate of recruitment is the best practical guide for action. A form of protest that has gained success in one case may fail in another because of various local differences.

Antiwar protesters have been criticized for interfering, for example, with the right of other students to have employment interviews on campus with representatives of Dow Chemical or the armed services. My own answer to this criticism has to take into account the concept of greater and lesser evils. I believe people are right to express publicly their moral outrage against a great corporation that claims that the illegality, immorality, brutality of a weapon it manufactures for the government is none of its concern. The inconvenience caused to students who must therefore go to an off-campus office for interviews is inconsequential by comparison. I also agree with the students who say that a university has no business giving recruiting space on campus to the military services when so many students, faculty, and citizens believe the government's war is illegal and abominable.

The charge that the protesting minority in a university interferes with the right of the majority to have a calm atmosphere for learning seems more complex to answer. It would be hard for me personally to participate with a very small minority in tying up an important university function for a prolonged period unless I had assurance from the recruitment of increasing numbers of students and faculty that the means were accomplishing the end. But someone else might bring up an example of a wrong so great and a student body so intimidated as to make me change this position and agree that an obstruction that in the short run could lead to nothing but a severe penalty might accomplish something important over the years.

Certain types of protest seem ethically wrong to me (others may disagree) and also likely to lose ground for a cause. When demonstrators invade an audience that has gathered to hear a certain speaker and by their uproar keep him from being heard, the audience is infuriated and so is the neutral public that reads about the episode in the news. This antidemocratic and useless interference with the rights of others seems quite different from a demonstration outside an auditorium against a speaker who is on his way in, in order to make a point to the public. I am against the forcible disruption of classes in schools and colleges. I am against the throwing of rocks and stink bombs and the roughing-up of deans, because these are acts of offensive not defensive violence. I am against the taunting of the police and the carrying of obscene signs because they impair the image of the cause, are really self-indulgences, and bring no benefit.

I'm opposed to the use of violence on principle, unless it is clearly in self-defense. Much of the world's misery is due to violence. The sooner we all abandon it and the threat of it, the more chance we have of saving mankind. It robs the perpetrator of much of his claim to the moral superiority of his cause. It brutalizes the victim as well as the perpetrator, for it gives both parties justification for increasing cruelty. It's a miserable way to try to usher in a better era. Practically, it is likely to backfire against the people who launch it, bringing support to the victims—as has been learned for example by President Johnson, Mayor Daley, and the presidents of several universities.

But some who would disagree could point out that I may be biased in taking this lofty stand through belonging to a favored racial and economic group. Certainly I feel that if we take the Declaration of Independence seriously, we must agree that black Americans have every moral right to violent revolution as a defense against constant aggression. But for such a small minority this would be disastrous and no black leader would ever advocate such a self-defeating action.

I am not a pacifist, though I respect the pacifist reasoning. I approved of going to war against Hitler and I would again if another Hitler appeared. If I were challenged to imagine a crisis here that could make me resort to violence, I'd say I would unhesitatingly join a revolution if an American President suspended the Constitution, dissolved Congress, or began throwing Americans into concentration camps without trial. I'm not claiming that these stands are absolutely right or best but only making my position clear.

What is never referred to by vigorous advocates of law

and order but is crucial for American moderates to understand is that almost all the violence in recent confrontations in the United States has been carried out by governmental forces. The rioting of desperate black people in the ghettos is most commonly touched off by an episode of police brutality (on top of ceaseless police abuse) and almost all the loss of life occurs among innocent black bystanders, caused by the indiscriminate violence of police and national guardsmen. At the Pentagon and at the Chicago convention young people who had every Constitutional right to protest were victims—not perpetrators—of violence. At some universities students have occupied buildings, a misdemeanor that is not directed against persons, is not violent, and is not outrageous since the buildings are not the personal property of anyone but are for students and faculty to use. Yet the students have been attacked with such patently unjustified violence at such universities as Columbia, Harvard, and California at Berkeley that large numbers of previously neutral students and faculty have been won to their side. And many universities have instituted the reforms for which the students demonstrated. Such results would not have occurred if the students or their demands had been unreasonable.

What about the young radicals who have been quoted as planning the destruction of the universities? When something like that is said it is usually the kind of overly dramatic rhetoric that some humorless radicals use to impress themselves, when they really mean a thoroughgoing reformation. On the other hand any student who literally means destruction is one of the very few who are living in a fantasy world. How would I know? I am a friend of hundreds of radical students and an acquaintance of thousands; the overwhelming majority are sensible and kindly.

In a sense the ultimate judgment about any dissent—how far people are morally and practically justified in going, in regard to which issues—is decided by history. Our American history books are able to glorify the dumping of tea into Boston Harbor and the Revolution not just because we are all now agreed that taxation without representation is tyranny but because our forefathers beat the redcoats over this issue. Otherwise the books would come to different conclusions. Yet this is not a cause for cynicism—about might making right—since the moral rightness of fighting tyranny in the Age of Reason was presumably what gave our forefathers the resoluteness that led to victory—right makes might.

Conscientious people caught between their distress at injustice and their distress at the thought of putting pressure on the authorities sometimes ask whether there isn't some comfortable formula that will tell them what position or what steps are morally justified. Of course there is no such answer, especially in a time of heightened social conflict—otherwise the conflict would never have arisen or it could have been quickly settled.

Each individual has to painfully make up his mind on the basis of how his conscience weighs the injustice, his own interests, and his estimated future peace of mind. And when events are moving as rapidly as now, he has to reconsider his position every week.

Is Labor Moving to the Right?

The poor who are unemployed or underemployed—both white and black—feel themselves outside American society, studies show. (Those most deprived are also emotionally depressed—from feelings of rejection and hopelessness.)

In the first part of this century as well as in the nineteenth century a considerable proportion of the employed laborers, many of whom were recent immigrants whose low wages bought only a poverty level of subsistence, also felt themselves outsiders on the American scene. They were underdogs. Intellectual radicals identified with them as such.

But as wages have gone up and as the Labor Establishment has become a powerful part of the Democratic Party, many labor union leaders and members have now become insiders with a vengeance. They are exaggeratedly conservative, respectable, patriotic, and highly critical of people who, according to their standards, don't conform. This is the insecurity felt by any individuals or groups who have recently reached a new level of status but can't quite believe yet that it is real or permanent. They express it as excessive loyalty and admiration for their new peers and superiors and as scorn for those at the level they have left behind. It is shown by people who have just entered their profession, at last, or joined the golf club. It helps explain why each ethnic group immigrating into America first had to take insulting abuse and then had to deal it out. It used to separate many middle-class black people from any identity with the poorer members of the race until they became aware of its significance and effect. It's an integral element of human nature—an aspect of the pecking order. It shows up in child development, too: Those who have just arrived in adolescence are often extremely intolerant of younger members of the family and want no reminders that they were ever like that. They cling to others of their age.

All levels of white society have participated in the abuse of black people; but the discrimination has been expressed with particular indignation by members of many unions and ethnic neighborhoods who feel most directly the imagined threat of black competition and identify most anxiously with the middle class. They believe that black people moving into their neighborhoods threaten them with loss of standards. They are fervent advocates of law and order. Opinion polls reveal that they believe blacks are asking greedily for everything—much more than their share—and that the government is unfairly giving it all to them. This despite the fact that, after fifteen years of supposed progress, most blacks are still penalized by exactly the same ghetto schools, same ghetto housing, same severe unemployment.

A majority of organized labor groups also backed America's Vietnam policy unequivocally. I've seen them help the police to attack war protesters. In the 1968 campaign significant percentages shifted their support from the Democratic Party to Nixon and Wallace. If such attitudes should prove to represent a persistent shift of organized labor and of ethnic groups away from the progressive end of the spectrum and into the exaggeratedly conservative end it would be one of the significant changes in American political history. Where would sufficient political pressure come from to advance the social welfare of those below a median income?

The prospect is disturbing. Black people, who generally have a deep cynicism about politics because they have never received any of the things that politicians promised, will have to be motivated to go a lot further in political organizing, along with the poorer whites, in order to bring to bear a pressure commensurate with their numbers, which at most constitute a minority.

The main hope for bold social progress will have to lie with the younger generation of all economic levels. I believe that the determination of youth to participate in the building of a more just and kindly nation and their readiness to support liberal and radical means will continue to increase. (Surveys now reveal the spirit of protest in half of all high and junior high schools.) I trust that enough of them will resist the normal drift to a more conservative political position after they acquire jobs and families.

Another hope is to find more effective ways—mainly through community organizing approaches—to change the perspectives of older people: to show white people of all economic levels that they don't need to fear the presence of black home owners in their neighborhood, black children in their schools, black workers in their industries and unions. A few neighborhoods and schools have set an example. Radical community organizers must find ways to show working people that war resisters are not betraying their sons in the armed services but are trying to save their lives, that student protesters are working for a better education for all, that young radicals will gladly help labor to get higher real wages.

If liberals and radicals decide that union labor and the police are their permanent enemies, they'll find plenty to justify their hatred and will foster further mutual antagonism. But if they can avoid the paranoid temptation and realize that these people—like all others—are reacting to deeply felt anxieties, they'll find where the constructive efforts should go.

Stormy Years Ahead

I don't pretend to see the full picture of the next half dozen years, but I think certain forces and trends are predictable.

I don't believe that President Nixon will soon face what is required to end the war in Vietnam: abandoning our puppet regime and our plan to keep control of South Vietnam. Therefore the disaffection of youth, the deterioration of the cities, the neglect of health, education and welfare will all continue. Even if the President could find substantial funds, his record suggests he would not spend them for the cities and for poverty, since he has consistently shown a conviction that the people's problems will be solved by industry if government will maintain conditions favorable to industry.

Black people will continue to be deeply frustrated because their exaggerated poverty will continue, the implementation of Black Power programs will be slow and difficult, civil rights and school integration will proceed at a snail's pace as usual because officials will be even more ambivalent than in the past. The righteous anger of black people will intensify and result at least in sporadic outbreaks of rage. Yet as elections and polls clearly show, a majority of America's citizens has decided to ignore the injustices done to black people and instead to encourage the police to repress them more drastically than before in the name of law and order.

Since the police and National Guard will be able to apply much greater fire power than black people can and follow it up with mass arrests, false accusations, and long prison terms (as they are already doing to the Black Panthers all over the United States), will black people generally control their rage, organize, and bide their time? Or will many choose to die fighting? I myself hope that during the intensified reaction of today they will avoid open confrontations, which the police will use as provocation. I also hope that young black people in universities and schools will curb their natural impulse to separate themselves from white fellow students, so that the two groups can learn to know and trust each other to a degree and to build alliances for the dangerous present and a possibly more constructive future.

If large scale riots occur, would most of the segments of The Establishment be in favor of or object to the use of the police and the armed forces to impose a national state of emergency with concentration camps? Though this may sound fantastic, many black and white radicals don't think it is out of the question in view of the mood of the country.

Young people at the high school as well as the university level will become outraged in increasing numbers as the evils and the harshness of the repression mount. Their protests will continue to anger citizens, editors, legislators, and officials. Some older people, remembering the severity and effectiveness of the repression of the 1950s, expect young people of the 1970s to be intimidated too. I disagree. I've learned both as teacher and as friend that they cannot be intimidated. Bullying from congressional committees, officials, and the police will only confirm them in their radicalism and make them more courageous. They will tell the truth to congressional inquisitors. They will, incidentally, encourage liberals of the older generation to be a little braver too.

By 1972 I believe that President Nixon's failure to solve any problems will result either in a more reactionary government under a George Wallace or a more liberal and humanitarian one under a McGovern. I think that the latter is more likely because Nixon will have moved far enough to the right to rob a reactionary candidate of most of his ammunition, and still it won't have worked. And I think that there will be sufficient votes to elect a McGovern among the old liberals, the young people, the black people, and enough middle-of-the-roaders who have become disillusioned with conservative slogans, inflation or unemployment, a disappointing standard of living, misery and hatred on all sides.

A liberal Democrat will be able to heal some scars and improve the people's welfare. But he or his successor will become involved in further imperialist adventures, unless a radical party is by then gaining enough strength to threaten the Democratic Party from the left and push foreign policy in the opposite direction.

The healthy way for a radical party to develop would be from local grass roots, beginning in places where the need is greatest. It should be an all-year, every-year effort, involved in all kinds of community organizing, not just concerned with electoral politics. It should interest itself in every issue that is of real concern to the district, hold discussions to clarify the needs and views of citizens, offer leadership, focus pressures on local officials and organizations that control the life of the community. In a poor neighborhood the crucial job might be to help families to get better service from welfare or education departments. In a less deprived neighborhood the primary need may be for real estate tax relief or health care.

Pioneering work to organize the most disadvantaged communities—by helping the residents to find political, technical and occupational ways to help themselves—has already been carried out in recent years in different areas of the nation by dedicated young community organizers, who have lived in poverty areas at poverty levels to do so. Some of these programs have eventually taken the form of an independent local political party. Others have constituted themselves as people's community unions, in order to bargain with the governmental, commercial, educational, professional and labor organizations in the locality. When a national radical new party emerges, these local community organizations will be able to join it.

I'll list some urgent domestic programs that I think should be stressed by a radical party:

Black people must be given freedom, equality, and dignity by a variety of remedies that attempt frankly to make up for past injustice. There should be fair employment laws, fair housing laws, school integration laws, *strictly enforced*. Massive aid to education will be essential, focused on the schools of the poor. There must be the best of schooling or job training for those adult individuals who left school without these essentials. To make up for past discrimination there ought to be subsidization of the purchase of housing, stores, small industry, and farms by black people.

In regard to agriculture it is wicked for the United States government to be restricting crops at a time when there are more hungry people on the earth than there have ever been before, when there are many hungry people in the United States, and at a time when our former huge stockpiles of surplus foodstuffs have dwindled. We should be trying to raise enough food to see that all world needs will be met. We can afford to pay our farmers for doing this.

Poor tenant farmers, of the South particularly, are being displaced by machinery and are moving to the cities where their skills count for nothing and where many of them become chronically unemployed and depressed. Instead they should receive government assistance so that they could buy their own farms and live on them more comfortably and a lot more happily than as welfare recipients.

We should be starting on a massive housing program for low income people (instead of the token programs we've had)—new apartments and houses and the rehabilitation of old apartments and houses. One emphasis should be on creating neighborhoods with all the ingredients for good living: space, dignity, quiet, greenery, recreation, cultural activities, schools, stores, ready transportation to work. The other emphasis should be on occupant ownership, occupant responsibility.

We have only just recognized that the aged should receive decent medical care as a right rather than as charity. In a few rich states the poor in younger age brackets are beginning to receive some medical assistance. But we are far behind a majority of the industrialized nations of Europe in providing or even thinking of providing good all-round care for everyone as a human right. How can we advocate less?

We need greatly to increase federal aid to education, in order to bring our more deprived schools up to adequacy —in the ghettos, in the South, in rural areas. We also need rapidly increasing facilities at the junior college, college, and professional school level.

I feel that parochial schools and church universities should receive the same aid as others, provided they meet standards and avoid discrimination; otherwise students in these schools are simply discriminated against in the quality of their education in order to satisfy the community's anti-Catholic prejudice.

We should adopt the guaranteed annual income. It ought not be thought of as a substitute for employment for every worker, at the highest level of which he is capable. But once and for all it would put an end to the despair of the worst levels of poverty and the ignominy of welfare and charity. There is no financial or moral reason why a society as wealthy as ours should not assure this level of subsistence to all its citizens. It would be a bargain, too, in ensuring more stable families, fewer neglected children, less delinquency and crime, fewer unschooled, untrained people in the next generation.

The kinds of programs I have listed may sound extravagant to some but this is because in America we have had a traditional prejudice against them—that they were socialistic and detrimental to the free enterprise system or that they would bankrupt us. Actually, not only the Communist countries but the democratic welfare states of Europe, with far less wealth than the United States, have long since provided such services.

When America has extricated itself from the war and all nations agree to begin to limit armament, there will be tens of billions of dollars available to bring America up to the decency level. In fact it will be essential then, in order to avoid a depression, to get to work on constructive governmental programs—for housing for the poor, for schools, for hospitals and clinics—to take up the slack in industry and labor. Production for private consumption alone could no longer keep America busy even if it were desirable.

V
Education for What?

I attended an assortment of schools and universities all of which went at teaching with traditional methods, though I took the third and fourth grades in an open-air school in a tent where we wore outdoor winter clothes and sat in felt bags. I assumed I had received the finest education until I met, as a student at the New York Psychoanalytic Institute, Caroline Zachry, a leader in progressive education and also a student of psychoanalysis. She told me about the deeper educational values of class projects, of learning by feeling and doing, of student discussions of the human relations of the class itself. After I better understood these dimensions of education I realized that they had always been found essential, on a pragmatic basis, in medical education. In my last dozen years of teaching, at Western Reserve University Medical School, I participated in bold experiments in applying the principles of progressive education more deliberately to medical education. They worked well. These same principles belong in all kinds and levels of schools, I am convinced.

There are many distinct sides of education. To remember the product of seven times eight, to find the greatest common denominator, to understand relativity, to teach math to second-graders, to head a university department of mathematics—all are aspects of one subject, mathe-

matics; all are quite different skills, learned by entirely different methods.

I'm not going to try to cover all aspects of education. What I want to focus on is the contrast between various philosophies of education, to show how they may contribute to or interfere with the job of teaching people how to get along in life and how to find the truth—the two ultimate purposes of education in my view.

In this discussion I criticize the overly intellectual approach of many teachers, especially at the university level; but I criticize from within the circle, being an emeritus professor and, I think, an intellectual.

Primitive Parental Education

We're apt to assume that most of learning takes place through an intellectual exchange in schools and universities, though of course this isn't so. Most of our body skills, language skills, human relations skills, which are the foundation for any work, are learned before kindergarten. And what occurs in the classroom is dependent on emotional and interpersonal factors as much as on academic procedures.

In "primitive" parts of the world there haven't been schools but there has always been very active teaching of occupational skills by parents. This parent-child teaching is worth looking at because it tells us a lot about the human dynamics of all education: A boy from the age of three has an overwhelming drive to be like his father and to achieve in a simple society his father's very visible skills, whether fishing, hunting, raising crops, or herding cattle. Until he is allowed to help his father he practices make-believe. His father will take pride in training him as soon as custom says this will be worthwhile. A girl is impatient to assume her mother's roles as caretaker of babies, preparer of food, weaver of clothes, and her mother will be delighted to show her the way. Educational motivation is essentially emotional and personal: love, admiration, identification (child with parent and parent with child); later, rivalry adds a different dimension.

187

When a society becomes complex enough to want to record its business transactions, legends, and religion, it has to get its children into school. Then a lot must change in regard to the content of education. Unfortunately—and unnecessarily, I believe—the spirit of education is apt to change, too.

The Drift to Pedantry

The tendency of formal schools through the centuries has been to focus (after reading and writing are learned) on the memorizing of definitions, tables, facts, dates, moralisms. Wisdom is assumed to come from the knowledge accumulated by the religious prophets and the philosophers of the past. A classic example is the traditional education of a Moslem youth in an Arab village: He spends years memorizing the Koran; the eventual accomplishment of this feat will prove to the community that he is not only an educated but a moral man. In America in colonial times there was a strong emphasis on the reading, writing, and memorizing of moral and religious maxims.

Though we know now that memorizing is not a generally effective approach to wisdom and that old knowledge is being superseded so fast that it is often a hindrance, many mediocre teachers are still inclined to ask their students to memorize facts and the opinions of their teachers or of scholars of the past.

A principal reason for this is that teachers, particularly at the university level, are most often intellectuals by temperament. As such they may easily lose sight of the real-life meaning of an activity because of a preoccupation with the abstractions beyond it, that is, with concepts, with words, with forms. And their natural inclination is to give their own distilled wisdom to their students rather than think about what students are interested in and how they actually learn.

So textbooks start with definitions, which have no meaning for the student at this point, instead of ending with them. Biology starts with the paramecium, instead of with the human body, which is of natural concern to youths. Psychology starts with the neuron rather than with the urgent questions of young people about themselves. At graduate school level there is the tradition of the Ph.D. thesis for inculcating the scholarly approach. But the thesis is sometimes permitted to be concerned with a topic so worthless to humanity that it sounds like a joke; yet this is acceptable as long as all the forms are scrupulously observed. As a result, the Ph.D. thesis can foster a smug pedantry that helps to unfit a scholar for teaching others or even for getting along with people.

Child-Centered Education

In America in the twentieth century there have been two educational movements at the elementary level, designed to get the focus off the imparting of strictly academic skills by the teacher, off the requirements that the school lays down for its students, onto the child himself, how he learns, how he can be helped to mature.

The central concept of the Montessori method, brought

to the United States from Italy in 1907, was that a young child of three or four will respond with intense curiosity and enthusiasm to all kinds of sensory impressions. When guided into the task of responding in a disciplined way to these impressions (sorting sixty-four spools of various colors and shades, for instance) he will work eagerly to master the job. A long series of proven exercises over a period of two or three years will lead him into the three Rs by five or six.

The progressive education philosophy of Dewey, Parker, and Kilpatrick, which superseded the Montessori method in America, added further breadth and depth to child-centered education. There were a number of related concepts: Children don't have to be forced or even strictly guided; they will learn eagerly if the material is suitable, making their own use of it. They will advance their emotional and social as well as their intellectual maturity by creative activities including those carried out in cooperation with each other. Spontaneity and initiative are valuable to the individual and to society, so should be fostered. The learning of the various academic skills (reading, writing, mathematics, social studies) can be linked to a lively central project (American Indians in the third grade, for instance), which gives these skills a real-life meaning and excitement. Nonacademic activity related to the central project is valuable: painting, building models, trips to libraries, museums, industries. The children, in small groups, can help to select, plan, and carry out subprojects. The teacher encourages democratic discussion and decision, under his leadership, and allows the group to make mistakes that are not dangerous. This is learning by doing; it fosters cooperation, responsibility, democracy. Even the arguments and fights between members of the class and expressions of intolerance are considered grist for lively discussions of human nature. This is learning by feeling. Other aspects are the adaptation of the materials and methods to individual children with different degrees of intelligence and readiness by means of great flexibility in the program and by small classes, the substitution of conferences with parents in place of arbitrary report cards, the inclination to pass children to the next grade even though, in some cases, they have not succeeded in covering the year's work. The last is based on research which showed that these children who stayed with their classmates, by being promoted anyway, made more progress the next year than if they were discouraged by being left back.

In the high school years, though there is usually more emphasis on academic subjects, there can still be projects related to the outside community, which evoke student initiative and cooperation. The dynamic teacher welcomes the inclination of students to relate the topics that come up in literature, history, and science to their own everyday lives through discussions, for example, of the reasonableness or unreasonableness of certain parental rules, or of the pros and cons of current adolescent customs. The assumption still holds in high school that the most usable knowledge is gained by being lived and felt. Another assumption is that a likeable teacher's acceptance of each child inspires him with some of the teacher's ideals and helps him to accept his ever-changing adolescent self.

The Attacks of the Authoritarians and Intellectuals

Modern American education took its worst battering when the Soviet Union launched the first two Sputniks in 1957 and shattered America's complacency about being first in everything. The nature of this reaction should be understood because it will surely be repeated in the future. There was a sudden unleashing of hostility and scorn, by two groups particularly. One was the citizens of authoritarian personality (newspaper and magazine editors were their most vocal spokesmen) who had been bothered all along by what they considered the permissiveness of modern education, its emphasis on pleasure of learning, its lack of arbitrary discipline and of arbitrary standards of achievement. The authoritarian is convinced that ultimately people have to be controlled or activated by some form of intimidation—whether they are children, subordinates, a minority group, or the national enemy—in contrast to the democratic faith that people have good motives which only need the right stimulation and discussion to be mobilized.

The other prominent critics were a variety of intellectuals (overlapping with the authoritarians)—a majority of them on university faculties—who heaped scorn on such nonacademic subjects in high school as driver training, band, business English, typing, and life adjustment—particularly the last. Another accusation (made without supporting evidence) was that bright children were being submerged in a sea of mediocrity—an unfair reproach since modern educators, unlike the old, strive for the maximum flexibility possible in meeting each child's readiness.

Several of the critics whose views were most widely published were in agreement that French education was the model of excellence that America should strive to copy. They pointed to the precise and thorough knowledge that a French *lycée* student of literature, for example, acquires under relentless, authoritarian instruction. (A French high school principal, asked by an American reporter if it was true that French students are not encouraged to be spontaneous in discussion, replied, "We have no interest whatsoever in our students' opinions.") But the American critics took no notice of factors other than the superior erudition of French students (which, incidentally, I envy, too) that surely must be considered if educational systems are to be compared: I think of such matters as the proportion of young people offered higher education, the scientific and literary creativity of the two countries, their political maturity. French universities admit only one in twenty young people, compared to one in two in America, which means that the average French university student is the equivalent of an American Phi Beta Kappa scholar. If Nobel prizes can be used as one rough index, I would say that modern America has done creditably in science, medicine, and literature, certainly as well as France. France has had recurrent difficulty for two centuries in establishing a stable system of self-government. It was ironic also that just when the American critics were advocating a French type of education, there was a French education commission in America inquiring how this country managed to carry so many students so far.

To me the most significant aspect of this attack by academic intellectuals on America's schools was the evidence that they put all their faith and pride in the intellect. I believe that this attitude can lead human beings as far astray as an overweening pride in family or race.

The attack also reveals the anxiety of intellectuals at the prospect that feelings might be recognized and even be given a place in the curriculum. For the intolerance of feelings is a significant part of the make-up of many intellectuals. In medical schools it is the more intellectual researchers (as well as the more authoritarian surgeons) who are particularly upset by suggestions that the psychological and humane aspects of medicine should be taught in all the various clinical departments, in addition to the department of psychiatry—so that doctors in all specialties will recognize their patients' feelings and emotional needs. When I was a part-time school physician and recommended a one-hour conference in the fall with each homeroom teacher, to briefly review the physical and emotional problems in her class, the teachers in the primary grades, who were more concerned with the whole child, were enthusiastic. But the high school teachers, who were specialists in subject matter—and of a high academic caliber in that particular school—sent a disapproving message through the principal that they didn't have time. Not one hour per year.

Why do I make such an issue about overintellectualization? There is a sort of competition between the head and the heart for the control of each human being's actions. If the head becomes too dominant, by upbringing and education, the heart dries up. A more direct way to say this is that intellectuality—dealing with life in terms of abstract concepts—is often built up as a defense, as a protection, against the discomfort of feelings. Some highly intellectual individuals are hardly aware of other people's emotions or of their own. (The absent-minded professor is the comic exaggeration of this trait.) Such people may be thoughtlessly unkind or at least very difficult to live with, and their children are apt to develop the same impersonalness, by identification and also as protection. In their professional occupations they make those of us who are their clients uncomfortable by turning their backs on our feelings. As government officials—in housing or health or welfare—they can do extensive harm by ignoring the human needs of the millions they affect with their decisions. As teachers in schools and universities they can dehumanize—at least slightly—every student who sits in their class. Some psychologists and sociologists, who have chosen careers which would seem intended to bring them closer to man, presumably for his benefit, use their professionalism to hold man at a distance while they dissect him with an ill-disguised scornfulness. As more schooling becomes essential for more people, the importance of counteracting overintellectuality becomes greater, too.

In response to the attacks on American education by intellectual and authoritarian critics there was a move in some school districts "to cut out the frills and get back to fundamentals." A man was elected State Superintendent of Schools in California who campaigned on a platform of going back to the McGuffey Readers of the nineteenth century. The Montessori method was revived and spread rapidly because it appeared to somewhat intellectual and authoritarian parents as more disciplined, more academic, less concerned with the child's emotional and social development than nursery schools of the American tradition. The federal government appropriated generous sums for schools for the first time, but not for general improvement. The purpose was to strengthen the teaching of science in high schools—on two unsupported assumptions: (1) that more and better teaching will steer more students into science as a career and (2) that the security of the country depends on a greater focus on science. It could have been argued that what was needed was more history, philosophy, religion, and human relations, so that men's ability to get along with one another might catch up with their ingenuity in destruction.

A different wave of concern in the 1960s—about the large percentage of school dropouts—shifted the focus back to the problem of shaping education flexibly to the needs of students. Dropouts come mainly from families that have been demoralized by poverty and have never experienced the fruits of education. So the academic motivation transmitted from parents to children is low or nonexistent. In their early years most of these children experienced too little in the way of attention, conversation, stimulation. They rarely had a chance even to get out of their impoverished homes. They were never read to. As a result their intellects and their interest in learning are limited. They fall behind in school; then shame is piled on top of lack of interest. Their schools and teachers tend to be second- and third-rate. The adolescents see that many of the youths in the neighborhood who *have* finished high school aren't employed. Discouragement and adolescent rebelliousness encourage them to drop out. Feelings of discouragement and being an outsider are intensified by the inability to find a job and often lead to delinquency.

When local and federal officials faced up to this problem they turned to the few ingenious educators who had been successful in experiments in motivating dropouts to return to school. The solutions found by these experimenters came right back to the principles of progressive education: The educator must find the natural interests of the pupil, however elementary or nonacademic these interests are. Courses must be linked to real life situations in order to be meaningful. Each student must be helped to achieve some kind of success before too long, through being given projects and assignments commensurate with his ability, not pitted against an arbitrary standard that might be too high for him. This last point actually applies to students of *all* capabilities and to adults in all kinds of jobs: the courage and enthusiasm for tackling new assignments has to come in part from a sense of adequacy gained in coping with past assignments.

But those children who come from the most seriously deprived homes need more than just highly sympathetic teaching in the grades. That comes too late. They must be provided, in particularly good nursery schools, with the stimulating experiences that more favored children have earlier in abundance at home. More basically still, in order to respond at all, they must receive belatedly some simple affection and attention—from teachers and from parents. But parents who have felt rejected by society can't give much acceptance to their children. To put this more broadly, human beings can only give love if they receive it. Therefore when the emotionally deprived two-, three-, four-year-olds are taken into special nursery schools, their parents (mostly mothers without husbands) must be affectionately welcomed, too, and not just on special visiting days. They must be provided with a comfortable sitting room (with coffee) for getting acquainted and for discussions on subjects that concern them—child care, health and schooling, neighborhood problems, the utilization of welfare facilities. If in union they find strength, they may later organize militant action programs to arouse other citizens of the neighborhood to bring pressure on local government agencies. From an accepting staff the parents will gain a sense of belonging, of worth, of being likeable. Then they can identify with the teachers in becoming interested in what the children are doing and how they learn, provide them with simple playthings, answer their questions, take them on outings, read to them. Interest in their children's development and education, once aroused, will persist after their children go on to elementary school.

New Techniques and Ideas

It's often the academic ambitiousness of middle-class parents that particularly excites them about new teaching techniques that promise to move their children further, faster, and with less agony. That's why all of us parents should keep an eye on our own motives and be cautious in our enthusiasms.

The new approach in mathematics (when presented correctly) appears to be an example of genuine progress in that the pupils come to comprehend certain mathematical relationships not only earlier but more easily and deeply. The advantage is retained and forms the basis for further progress. The facility with which children advance with the new math really indicates that the old methods used for several thousand years, based on adults' presumptions rather than on experiments, were actually slowing down children's mathematical progress. This example shows that all teaching concepts need to be challenged.

The experiments in teaching three-year-olds to read are fascinating but they arouse in me several cautions. So far it has been necessary for each child to have an amount of adult attention and very special and expensive equipment far beyond what can be provided for large numbers of children. I am also made uneasy about the possible effect on a child's total personality of the focus of such intense concern by the teacher on the child as is shown in the motion picture demonstration of the method. The most important question is whether the acquisition of these skills at such an early age gives the child long-range advantages. Will he be a better reader at eight years? Will he have been able to learn other things which will make him a wiser child then and a more effective adult later? Experiments long ago showed that if children are held back in starting to learn to read until they are seven and in second grade, they will be reading and comprehending just as well at the end of that year as children of the same age who started reading at six years—and that less effort will have been required. Other experiments with identical twins showed that if you worked very hard at it you could teach one twin a certain physical skill somewhat earlier than the other would pick it up naturally, but that if you then ceased your drilling, he ceased to make further progress until about the time his twin caught up to him. In other words, there's a stage when a child is ready to acquire certain physical or mental skills and nothing permanent is gained by forcing a faster pace.

I don't mean that either of these particular examples proves that very early reading is not possible or advantageous, only that it will take years of experimentation before there are reliable answers.

It is possible that teaching machines will prove valuable in subjects involving memory, drill, and the intellectual mastery of certain kinds of concepts. They may be even superior to living teachers—at least for some students—in leading them, one small step at a time, at their own pace, into material that too easily becomes confusing when pushed by a teacher at a rate that is actually too fast. On the other hand, a machine, of course, cannot help a student to mature in human understanding or in functioning as a person or as a professional. It cannot teach a student how to organize his work, how to speak and write well, how to seek the truth in the library or the laboratory.

In such subjects as science and social studies teachers now encourage pupils to learn from attempting to solve real problems. They present to pupils the kinds of questions that have actually puzzled scientists in the past, the kinds of community challenges that have recently confronted government officials and experts in the social and health spheres. Students discuss possible solutions, carry out experiments, talk with officials. In these ways they learn not words, not theories, but how progress is actually made.

I consider it a good sign that high school and university students now care enough about their studies and the way their schools are administered that they want an official channel through which they can express their views. And they want assurance that their views will be given weight —in curricular and extracurricular decisions. Who should have a greater interest in the quality of his education than the consumer? And if he has the interest who has a better right to a voice?

I'd say that if a student is old enough to go to school— even elementary school—he's old enough to have ideas about his courses and to get benefit from discussing them with his teachers.

And if he is old enough to go to junior high school or above, his instructors and administrators should be able to profit from some of his ideas and he will mature in his sense of responsibility if he is given a role in decision-making.

This is not a new or frivolous idea. In certain universities in past ages the students themselves hired the faculty members.

Students are not asking that control in any area be turned over to them (with the exception of black students' demands in some schools that they have the greatest say in setting up a black studies program). They ask a definite voice, to be weighed along with the voices of faculty and administration.

Those who are startled by these proposals should not think of them simply as the demands of upstarts for unprecedented privileges. Students who are taught to accept everything that's handed out to them are learning how to be docile. That's not good training today for the citizens of a democracy. By and large I think students are good judges of teachers, courses, and of their own performances as students. They are not taken in by the overly friendly teacher or jokester who has little to offer. Nor do they object to difficult assignments if they feel they are really learning.

Abuse of Television

Television is potentially the most powerful medium for education—during the years of formal schooling and for the rest of life. It could explain to us the sciences and the technologies. In an exciting way it could open our narrow minds to the beauty, customs, contributions, and problems of peoples in other countries. It could make us more sharply aware of our own contradictory nature. It could vividly show us both sides of the controversial issues in our own country and in the world, issues that we now so quickly decide on prejudice alone. It could introduce a materialistic nation to the pleasures of the arts.

The power of television is recognized by governments outside America, which, if authoritarian, control it or, if democratic, delegate supervision to a nonpartisan, responsible board. Nothing shows more clearly America's reverence for money-making and mistrust of culture than the handing over of all the air waves to oily peddlers who sell hair dyes by wrapping them in stories of sentimentality or brutality, designed to appeal to the lowest levels of taste. It is as irresponsible as if all the universities and schools were turned over to advertisers with the right to choose the teachers, prescribe the content of courses, and interrupt the class every five minutes for another salesman. We cluck our tongues about Roman citizens being soothed with circuses while the Empire decayed but our misuse of television is quite comparable.

The False Dichotomy Between Practical and Liberal Arts Education

The high school teachers who look down on the teaching of typing and plumbing are indulging in snobbery. So are the university teachers who emphasize the distinction between the liberal arts program in the undergraduate years and the practical training of the professional school. There should be three major aspects of university education, I think: (1) The background in the arts and sciences, for general understanding, (2) training in occupational skills, and (3) actual work with people. These three aspects would best benefit all students in their preparation for working and living if they were taught in an integrated fashion. Girls who want to become beauticians should be able to learn how at high school. But they don't have to be deprived of a broader background on this account. They could have especially appealing history courses that start with the styles of dress, adornment, and cosmetics of different periods and that then, having caught the pupils' interest, would extend into other aspects of history and culture. Their courses in human relations, communication and mathematics could begin with aspects related to a beautician's needs and then branch out. When the different fields of learning for each individual's chosen field are tied together into a whole as much as possible, he will see their interrelationships, be more highly motivated to study those that at first seemed remote, acquire some breadth and depth and perspective in his approach to his own occupation.

The student at a liberal arts college needs regular opportunities, I believe, to experience the real world of jobs and ordinary people—under thoughtful supervision —to balance the theoretical concepts he is gaining in the classroom, whether or not he has yet chosen his life work, whether or not he is going on to graduate school. (A very few colleges already provide such experiences.) Otherwise all his theoretical concepts and overintellectualized attitudes may get in the way of his subsequent adjustment to life situations. An example with which I'm very familiar is the young woman who has taken child psychology theory at college without an opportunity to work with children. She may well have a more anxious, awkward time when she first takes care of her own baby, worrying about such disturbances as emotional deprivation, spoiling and insecurity, than the woman who has only finished high school but remembers well her care of the younger children in her family.

It has been known since medicine began to be based on

science a hundred years ago that the student cannot be satisfactorily educated with lectures and laboratories and books alone. He can learn a lot from these. But when he comes to deal with patients he doesn't know how to be a sound or satisfactory physician—what questions to ask, what to make of the answers, how to put the history together with the examinations to make a diagnosis, how to know what his patient's deepest concerns about his illness are, how to comfort him, whether or not he can cure him. A medical student has to be seeing patients at the same time that he is studying diseases in books and lectures. And he has to have a great deal of supervision from instructors in the clinics, who see the patients with him. If his instructors fail to make him aware of his patients' feelings—and of his own—his future patients may say of him, "He seems to know what he's doing, but I've never been able to talk to him about the things that really bother me."

I think that students preparing for all fields—law, business, teaching, journalism, government, the ministry, industry—need opportunities to work with ordinary people during their training, under the supervision of instructors well trained in human relations. This would counteract to a degree the tendency of many to become depersonalized, pompous, authoritarian, power-seeking.

The pattern in America of separating the four years of liberal arts undergraduate education from graduate school is inefficient, I think. If such background courses as history, composition, literature, psychology, sociology could be taught not only simultaneously with but also be integrated with the theory and the actual practice of the profession, the students would gain a broader perspective

on the potentialities of their profession. Also, by good
planning, it might be possible to eliminate one or two
years of the total course.

Teaching Morality

It's time, I believe, to reconsider the academic tradition
against teaching morality in courses devoted to other
subjects. Up through the Middle Ages academic institutions were established and administered by the Church
and it was assumed that religious teaching was the foundation of education. The Protestant Reformation ended
the monopoly control that the Catholic Church had previously exercised over the formulation of truth and the
administration of schools and universities. Increasingly
there was impatience with domination of thought by
any religion and an insistence on the right to free inquiry,
which reached a peak in the so-called Age of Reason in
the latter part of the eighteenth century and in the separation of church and state.

The teachers in the early colonial schools and universities of the United States were predominantly Protestant
ministers whose principal aim was to teach religious principles and to train more ministers, who became the next
leaders of the community. But the framers of our Constitution specified the separation of church and state here,
too. By the second half of the nineteenth century the
discovery of evolution and the development of various
behavioral sciences further weakened the authority of the

churches as educators. As the need for schools and universities mounted they were established increasingly by towns and states. Now the Supreme Court has forbidden in public schools even the vaguest of prayers.

Many parents, though they have personal codes of ethics, are quite uncertain these days about whether there is any general validity in religious teachings, morals, and ethics. Some clerics admit doubt about God. Many youths are left in a vacuum. They are offered no set of values either to subscribe to or to argue about. This situation amounts to a serious deficiency disease for a species designed to live by the spirit.

It's time for faculties to face the fact that the struggle to unshackle the search for truth from the domination of the Church has been mainly won. Science is not only free, it is sacrosanct—in the university, in government circles, and, as far as it is understood, among the public. It is worshipped idolatrously. Science and all its technological offspring are on the rampage, out of control of all considerations of morality. Their products and waste products are polluting the land, the rivers, and the air. Nuclear, bacteriological, and chemical weapons capable of depopulating the earth in a few hours accumulate perilously because no one knows a political formula for calling a halt. A space exploration program devoid of humanitarian value is syphoning off precious industrial, scientific, and financial strength. The resources going into the weapons and space races would be great enough to remake America and start the remaking of the rest of the world. Yet the teaching profession clings automatically to the old view that spiritual beliefs and morality are so different from the other inquiries of man—so disreputable academically—that they can't be considered freely in the ordinary classroom, in relation to the issues of today. They can be studied only in separate courses of ethics, philosophy, or history of religion. Faculty members and students have to go to political clubs and single-issue meetings and teach-ins to speak their convictions and hear the views of others. But surely the search for a morality that accords with man's nature and man's predicaments is as much a search for the truth as the search, for example, for the essential nutrients in his diet.

The teacher doesn't have to imply that his view of morality is the only tenable one. Besides, the student at the high school or university level can be counted on to resist indoctrination in the philosophical and moral spheres. The instructor can indicate various choices. I think it's important that he not only show his own beliefs, general and applied, but show the fervor of his convictions, for morality means little without the dimension of conviction.

Postcript

Man is in trouble—in an age when he could be enjoying paradise—for a bizarre variety of reasons. He has never—because of his conscience, of all things—been remotely able to face his disapproved characteristics: his rancorous hostility toward individuals and groups (which he ascribes to them instead), his greed and power-craving, the sultrier aspects of his sexuality. Yet now, because he has so belittled himself by means of his narrow sciences, he is no longer able to recognize an admirable side of himself either. He has lost much of his idealism and dignity.

Meanwhile technology has filled the gaps and become the worshipped tyrant. The environment is fouled. Things displace spirit. Education is pulled away from humanism. Affluent groups become not more altruistic but greedier. The very ingenuity and success of industry in the United States is what stimulates it to try to dominate the world. New weapons, piled high for security, threaten survival itself.

Through lifelong education man has to face more realistically his aggressiveness, his self-deceptiveness and the fact that such a large part of his motivation springs from the unconscious layers of his mind. Then he will be in a better position to control the emotional forces that now mislead and endanger him.

And he has to learn again that he is naturally endowed with a potential for idealism, spirituality, and creativity that are as real as any of his other abilities. They have to be utilized in order to keep the individual and society from demoralization.